'Smart, funny and absolutely fascinating. Lurking behind all that facial hair is an unexpectedly profound exploration of the way beliefs turn to rules and change the way we look and act. You'd think a man calling himself Mouse and writing about beards would be hiding something, but this book is wonderfully revealing about human nature.'

Cole Moreton, writer & broadcaster

'Despite not having a beard (the occasional pre-menopausal random chin hair aside) this is a hairy good read. Beard theology? I mean, who knew? A must-read for everyone from 70s-style Oxbridge chin-stroking theologians to church-in-an-industrial-unit hipster evangelicals.'

Revd Kate Bottley, priest in North Nottinghamshire & BBC Radio 2 presenter

'On the face of it, tracking the history and theology of men's facial hair throughout the Bible and the history of the Church may "be-a-rd-ifficult" concept for some of us to take seriously. But I "moustache-sure" you that it leads to an unusual yet intriguing read.

'Beyond the fuzz Mouse helps us to explore male identity, gender disparity, cultural appropriation and the contextualisation of the gospel. This book does not shortcut the issues, trim off the rough bits or split unnecessary theological hairs. Razor sharp in its wit and charm, it offers us a whisker-stop tour of all sorts of hairy and prickly issues.'

Dr Krish Kandiah, Founding Director of Home for Good & author of *God is Stranger* and *Paradoxology*

'Ever wondered about beards and their theology? No, me neither, but this little book has persuaded me that I should have. It is as informative as it is entertaining – read it, you won't regret it.'

Dr Paula Gooder, Chancellor of St Paul's Cathedral, London

'I love this hirsute "horrible history" of the Church. It's funny, enlightening and completely novel – which is some achievement given the history of Christendom!'

Revd Dave Tomlinson, vicar & author of *Black Sheep and Prodigals*

Beard Theology

Beard Theology

A holy history of hairy faces

As told by

THE CHURCH MOUSE

HODDER

First published in Great Britain in 2019 by Hodder & Stoughton
An Hachette UK company

This paperback edition first published in 2022

1

A CIP catalogue record for this title is available from the British Library

Paperback ISBN 978 1 529 31864 7
eBook ISBN 978 1 529 31865 4

Typeset in Sabon MT by Hewer Text UK Ltd, Edinburgh
Printed and bound in Great Britain by Clays Ltd, Elcograf S.p.A.

Hodder & Stoughton policy is to use papers that are natural, renewable
and recyclable products and made from wood grown in sustainable
forests. The logging and manufacturing processes are expected to
conform to the environmental regulations of the country of origin.

Hodder & Stoughton Ltd
Carmelite House
50 Victoria Embankment
London EC4Y 0DZ

www.hodderfaith.com

The beard signifies the courageous; the beard distinguishes the grown men, the earnest, the active, the vigorous.

St Augustine of Hippo

Contents

Preface

I stumbled upon the untold history of beards early in 2018 after spotting a novelty book on beards in a bookshop. I wondered, idly, whether anyone had written on the theology of beards. A small amount of research uncovered a rich seam from which to mine the golden nuggets of this book.

After discovering that Jesus almost certainly had a beard, I found that a cardinal had lost the papacy because of his beard and that beards have been, at the very least, a topic of comment from the time of St Augustine right through to the present day. My curiosity was well and truly sprouting and I set about more systematic research. Little did I know that this idle curiosity of one afternoon would grow into a minor obsession. The religious history of beards quickly became a religio-historical vortex from which a humble Mouse could not escape.

The stories I found and have gathered together in this book entertained and fascinated me, not least the fact that they exist at all – that anyone would have put serious thought into the theological virtues – or otherwise – of facial hair. And yet they have.

After reviewing the arguments made both for and against beards, all put forward with great sincerity and often with great fervour, it is extremely hard not to conclude that, after all, God probably does not care either way whether a man's (or a woman's, for that matter) face is hairy or smooth. God said to the prophet Samuel, 'The LORD does not look at the things people look at. People look at the outward appearance, but the Lord looks at the heart' (1 Samuel 16:7). It is extraordinary that, in the entire history of Jewish thought and Christian argument on the topic of beards, I have not found this verse quoted once. But, believe it or not, throughout history the whys and wherefores of the beard could not be so easily, ahem, brushed aside. People have lived and died, and the Church itself as we know it today has, in part, been shaped (and trimmed) by its beard theology. Yet, to us today, even giving it a few seconds' thought seems ridiculous.

Perhaps, in some small way, we will be drawn to the conclusion that some other issues about which religious people fall out with each other are probably not as important as they seem. God looks not at the outward appearance, but at the heart.

My hope with this work is, first, that it educates and entertains. I also hope that this education will include a realisation that we can all bring our presuppositions and assumptions with us when we engage in religious and political debates, and that we might still be doing this today in contemporary discussions on more substantial issues.

For those who read this and are inspired to continue reading on this topic, I heartily endorse Christopher Oldstone-Moore's *Of Beards and Men: The Revealing History of Facial Hair* and Allan Peterkin's *One Thousand Beards: A Cultural History of Facial Hair*, which were both essential research sources in the preparation of this work.

I would like to take the opportunity to thank Andy Lyon and the publishing team at Hodder and Stoughton for all their advice and support. Special thanks also go to Bishop Graham Kings, Paula Gooder and Miranda Threlfall-Holmes for taking the time to provide their views and comments on early drafts. Huge thanks also to the brilliant Dave Walker who was a pleasure to work with on the illustrations.

Finally, the biggest thanks must go to Mrs Mouse, who has lived with this strange obsession with an extraordinary degree of patience and fortitude.

Introduction

The history of the worldwide Church is as wonderful as it is surprising and mystifying. The Church began as a tiny band of poorly educated men and women in a backwater of the Roman Empire following a man who claimed to be God. Today, around one-third of the planet's population claims to be Christian. The journey between those two points is one of the greatest stories in history.

However, the Church has been divided on many issues in the two thousand or so years since Christ founded it on the rock of St Peter. The divinity of Christ, whether Jesus is physically or spiritually present in the bread and wine of Holy Communion, priestly celibacy, the role of women in the Church, and many more issues have risen to the fore in our own time to such a degree as to cause rupture, schism and even violence in the worldwide Church. Yet one issue has been under the surface through all these times, rarely breaking through to the headlines, but constantly fuelling the fire of division. Beards. To shave or not to shave, that is the question. Is a trim as good as a shave, and should the facial follicles be left to sprout as the Lord made them?

The story that unfolds in these pages is fascinating in its own right, but it is more than just a quirk of history. Beard theology is important. It matters precisely because it clearly does not matter. Yet, for centuries, the devout argued, often fiercely, over something that virtually nobody today would consider to be a point of any significance whatsoever. In its day, the issues of beard theology were considered worthy of debate alongside issues such as priestly celibacy, the nature of the sacraments and even the great debates on the divinity of Christ and the Trinity. Beards divided not just the worldwide Church, but also the societies they represented.

People argued about beards, taxed them, banned them and fought over them. Partly this was because they believed something about them. But, more importantly, it was about what beards represented. Beards were symbols of identities and social divisions that allowed people to display the difference between themselves and others in the way they looked. Identity politics has been alive and well for millennia, and beards have been part of that story.

For those of us who consider ourselves part of the Church, there are lessons to learn about how theological differences become entwined with a sense of self and identity, which in turn allows issues to escalate in their importance. It helps us understand that we do not approach Scripture, theology or church traditions from a position of neutrality. Such a position, in fact, has never existed.

So beard theology is important. Anyone who wishes to live in a more peaceful world, or to learn how to understand and accept differences, must pay attention to our beard history. Those who cannot learn from their beard history are bound to regrow it.

PART I
FOR GOD SO LOVED THE BEARD

1

Christ and the Beard of Life

Any discussion of the religious history of beards must surely begin with Jesus. For the world's 2.4 billion or so Christians, the example of Christ is the ultimate authority. His life is a guide for all to follow. Jesus lived a sinless life, the purpose of which was to save us from our sins. So, if you want to know whether beards are pleasing to God, we could start by considering the beard of our Lord.

We probably all believe that Jesus was a bearded man. But why, when there are no contemporary descriptions or images of him? What does the Bible have to say about beards and how did that influence the theology of the early church? The great fathers of the early church had a surprising amount to say on the subject of facial hair. The approach they took to the imitation of Christ and to the creation of their theology is part of the foundation of the theology of the modern Church. It can help us reflect on the foundations of our own theology.

The beard of our Lord

Christ's face is one of the most recognisable images in the world. Whether it appears in an exquisitely painted fresco, a cartoon on a T-shirt or the burnt crust of our toast, we are still able to make it out distinctly as the face of Jesus. And that face has a beard. We all know what Jesus looked like. Our image of Jesus has a beard because the historical Jesus had a beard.

There are no written descriptions of Jesus from anyone who could have met him, however. Nothing in the Bible describes his physical appearance. Most confusingly, the earliest surviving images of Christ depict him as clean shaven. It was not until the fourth century that the first bearded Jesus was depicted in art and it was another century before this became the dominant image. The familiar picture of the pale-skinned, blue-eyed, long-haired Jesus with a flowing beard cannot be an authentic representation of a first-century Palestinian Jew. Well, certainly not the pale skin and blue eyes bit. But what about the beard? Why have we decided that Jesus had a beard, in the absence of any primary evidence?

Let us set off on our journey to discover the holy history of hairy faces with the holiest and hairiest of them all, and work out how Jesus got his beard.

The saviour formerly known as ⳨

The earliest picture of Jesus that the world's archaeologists have uncovered dates from around AD 250. To our best guess, that would be a little more than two hundred years after Jesus was crucified by the Romans just outside Jerusalem. The earliest Christians did not make images of Christ. This was for two very good reasons, the first being that the Bible told them not to. One of the Ten Commandments says, 'You shall not make for yourself an image in the form of anything in heaven above or on the earth beneath or in the waters below' (Exodus 20:4), which seemed pretty clear in the traditional Jewish and early Christian interpretation.

The second reason was equally compelling. Painting a Christian image was likely to get you killed. After the Great Fire of Rome in AD 64 the Emperor Nero blamed the Christians and they became a group to which it was dangerous to belong. For around two hundred years, varying degrees of persecution acted as an effective deterrent to those who may have wished to own and enjoy Christian images, as well as to those who might have been employed to create them.

As a result, the earliest representations of Jesus were symbolic and ambiguous. They included:

- **A FISH** – the Greek word 'ichthus' forms an acronym for 'Jesus Christ, Son of God, Saviour'. It quickly became one of the most widely used Christian symbols and survives in the form of badges, wristbands, car stickers and hipster Christian tattoos to this day;

- **A PEACOCK** – this one has not survived. It was based on the ancient Greek belief that the flesh of the peacock did not decay after death. The peacock was associated with immortality and was adopted by early Christians as a figurative illustration of Jesus;

- **THE ANCHOR** – this one survives in popular worship songs that ask God to be our anchor, but its meaning is widely misunderstood. In ancient times the anchor was a symbol of safety and was adopted by Christians as a sign of hope;

- **THE STAUROGRAM** (which looks a bit like a cross with a long P forming the upright). It is a combination of the Greek letters T and P and was simply an abbreviation of the word 'stauros', the Greek word for cross. It is used in a number of early copies of the New Testament.

CHRISTIAN SYMBOLS

FISH   PEACOCK   ANCHOR   STAUROGRAM

RAINBOW STRAP

SANDAL   QUICHE   GUITAR   BEARD?

After a couple of hundred years, however, images depicting Jesus himself started to appear.

The early Jesus

One place where we find some of the earliest Christian art is the catacombs of Rome. The catacombs were originally a burial place for Christians lower down the social scale. Later, they became the last resting place for Christians of all stripes, from the lowest to the very highest. The remains of popes from the third century are buried there and are still visited today by pilgrims seeking a connection to the early saints.

As the social, and therefore financial, status of those buried there rose, so did the level of luxury in which their earthly remains were laid to rest. The catacombs became decorated with fine frescos which formed an artistic commentary on the character of the souls upon whom they looked down.

On the many miles of underground tombs around Rome, the image of Christ as the Good Shepherd appears more than a hundred times, including the earliest known depiction of Jesus in the catacombs of San Callisto on the Appian Way. The wall painting there is well preserved for its age and shows Jesus as a young man with a lamb around his shoulders and carrying a pot to feed the other lambs, which gather around his feet. He is wearing white robes, and there can be no mistake at all that there is not a single hair upon his divine chin. His upper lip is unquestionably bare.

To understand how the image of Jesus that we know came about, we need to understand a fundamental truth about how Jesus has been perceived by people throughout the ages: we see Jesus as we expect him to be. We see him through the lens of our own cultural norms and expectations. The reason the Good Shepherd on the wall of the San Callisto catacomb has no beard is because he was painted by a Roman who depicted Christ as he imagined him to be, with all the cultural reference points of Roman society and mythology intact.

The most obvious giveaway that the Jesus in the catacombs is not a historically accurate portrayal is those white robes he is wearing: a Roman tunic. The Hebrew carpenter in occupied Palestine would never have worn traditional Roman dress. He is also shown with olive skin and short hair – an idealised Roman youth, according to the traditional artistic style of the period.

We might imagine the commission given to this Roman painter to have been something like this:

PATRON: Hi there, are you good at painting frescos in catacombs?

PAINTER: Me? Seriously? I'm the best catacomb fresco painter this side of Hadrian's Wall, mate!

PATRON: Very well, my good fellow. Could you paint Jesus as the Good Shepherd for me in the San Callisto catacomb on the Appian Way?

PAINTER: You want me to paint who? As the good what, now?

PATRON: Jesus. As the Good Shepherd.

PAINTER: OK, I'm fine with the shepherd bit, but who is this Jesus chap? Friend of yours, was he?

PATRON: Sort of. He is the Son of God. Our risen Lord and Saviour. He died then rose to new life and is now reigning at the right hand of God in heaven, until he comes again to judge the living and the dead.

PAINTER: Right. I'll take your word for that. Can you just tell me what he looks like?

PATRON: Ah, no, not really. No idea, to be honest. You'll be the first person ever to paint him. Or at least in the future your painting will be the earliest one to survive.

PAINTER: Not a problem. Nil problemum, as they say in the forum. You tell me what he was like and I'll paint someone who I think might look like that character.

PATRON: Good idea. He was fully divine and fully human at the same time. He lived a sinless life and brought good news of the coming of the kingdom of God. He was then betrayed and crucified in shame. He was the Lamb of God and a Good Shepherd to his people.

PAINTER: Well, why didn't you just say he was a demi-god! I've been painting them for years. I tell you what, I'll just do you a Hermes, but take off the winged shoes and helmet. OK? I often do him carrying a lamb anyway, so that works as a good shepherd. Hermes brought messages from the gods to humans – you say your chap brought good news from God. He was a handsome lad, too.

PATRON: Sounds perfect! When can you start? You'd better hurry, I'm starting to feel a little poorly.

The Roman painter attempting to paint a man who was the Son of God had plenty of reference points from his own culture to borrow from. While the resulting image would not be historically accurate, it would at least mean that those viewing the pictures would understand the language of the painting. Good skin, firm calf muscles and white robes were all part of the normal artistic interpretation of the plethora of half-human, half-divine figures in Roman mythology. They were naturally borrowed to represent the Jesus whose real image had already been lost to posterity, but whose divinity was to be expressed.

Hermes and Dionysus were commonly borrowed images. Dionysus had a strong link as the god of wine, as Jesus said he was the vine and his followers were the branches. Sol Invictus, the Invincible Sun, was also commonly used. Worship of Sol Invictus was formally instituted by the Emperor Aurelian in AD 228, around the time when images of Jesus started to appear. The obvious links between the Light of the World and the Invincible Sun were so strong that this image was even used as the basis of a mosaic in the Vatican in the third century.

In the Basilica di San Pietro, a grotto under the Vatican, a wonderful ceiling painting shows Christ as the sun god. He is riding a Roman chariot and has rays of light emanating from his head. The painting is decorated with the vines of Dionysus around it, making it a classic example of Roman art bringing its own language and history into Christian art.

So the Jesus seen by early Christians in Rome was one who looked an awful lot like Roman gods and heroes. And they never had beards.

Symbolic Jesus

When looking back at these images, it is easy to see them as a kind of corrupted art form – taking non-Christian images and pretending that Jesus looked like a kind of Roman god. However, that is a very modern interpretation. At the time, the artists would not have seen their job as to represent what Jesus actually looked like. They were trying to tell a story with the images. They were hoping that meaning would come through the artwork. To do this, there needed to be a form or artistic language that the artist and the viewer shared. The traditions of Roman mythology presented those opportunities. When they showed Jesus as the sun god, it was not meant to say that is what he actually looked like. It was simply a way of showing him as immortal.

For this reason, most of the earliest images of Jesus show him beardless. Another third-century fresco in Rome, in the same San Callisto catacomb, shows Jesus raising Lazarus from the dead, with Jesus looking every bit the Roman nobleman. Even the only other known third-century image of the adult Jesus, found in the wall of the Dura-Europos Church in Syria and showing the healing of the paralytic, appears to show Christ without any facial hair.

It is not until the fourth century that we start to find images of Jesus with a beard. Even after that, we find as many beardless Christs in paintings as we do bearded ones. Fascinatingly, we sometimes find the same artist representing Christ in the same artwork with *and* without a beard in two different places.

The Church of Sant'Apollinaire Nuevo in Ravenna, Italy, was built by the Ostrogoth King Theodoric the Great as his palace chapel in AD 504. It was later re-consecrated by the Byzantine Emperor Justinian I in 561. It is a UNESCO World Heritage Site and is filled with dazzling mosaics.

Two sequences of mosaics are of particular interest. One sequence shows Jesus' life and ministry, including many of his miracles; the other shows Jesus' betrayal, trial and death on the cross. Jesus is wearing the same clothing throughout. In the first sequence he has no beard and it shows him very much in the tradition of a Roman demigod. However, in the second, created by the same artist at the same time, his beard and hair grow steadily throughout the sequence until he is fully bearded.

As with our earlier images, the artist is less concerned with portraying a lifelike picture, and more with presenting an image with meaning. In this case, the artist wants to show Christ as different from the men around him during his earthly ministry. He is also different from the angels and other heavenly creatures when he ascends. There was a tradition at this time of Jesus growing old and weary with his sorrows during the latter stages of his earthly ministry. The beard is intended to show that this is later in Jesus' life than the earlier pictures and that he has taken on the troubles of the world. So they put a beard on him.

We can say without much hesitation that we know at least one thing that Jesus didn't look like – a Roman god. We can also state, without beating around the bush and trying our very best to get straight to the point, that Jesus unquestionably had a long beard.[1] Not only did he have a long beard, but

---

[1] I'm going out on a bit of a limb here – we can't know exactly how long his beard was, but we can be sure he didn't cut it, so it is reasonable to think it must have been pretty long.

he also considered it an essential part of his faith, in the same way as was observing the Sabbath and eating kosher food.

We know all this because Jesus was an observant Jew and all observant Jews in his time had long beards. They had long beards for the same reason that they observed all of the rest of Old Testament legal code: because their Scriptures told them to as part of the law given to them by Moses to keep them holy before God.

Beards of the Bible

The Torah is the Jewish law that governs many aspects of life for Jewish people. It is known to Christians as the first five books of the Bible: Genesis, Exodus, Leviticus, Numbers and Deuteronomy.

It starts with the beautiful poetry of the Genesis accounts of the creation of the world. It continues with the familiar stories of Cain and Abel, Noah's ark, Moses, Joseph (of technicoloured dreamcoat fame) and much more besides.

But then it gets firmly stuck into a very long legal code. For this reason it is not recommended that new readers of the Bible start at the beginning and work their way through. You get off to a flyer with the Genesis and Exodus stories, enjoying the prose, only to be bitterly disappointed by page after page of, 'it is forbidden for . . .', and detailed descriptions of precisely how to bring your grain offering to the Lord.[2]

It is in this legal code in Leviticus that we find a particular prohibition of relevance to our narrative. In chapter 19, right after we are told not to eat meat with blood still in it and not to practise divination or seek omens, we are told, 'Do not cut the hair at the sides of your head or clip off the edges of your

---

[2] Leviticus 2, just in case this is applicable to you.

beard' (Leviticus 19:27). It is only a short instruction before the author continues with a prohibition against getting tattoos. In the Jewish tradition, there is a rich history of interpreting the Scriptures, often written down as the Mishnah. This verse has consistently been interpreted as meaning that shaving is forbidden. It is followed in chapter 21 of Leviticus with another prohibition on priests not to shave their head or their beard. It is for this reason that Orthodox Jews, both today and in Jesus' time, have long beards. But we are offered no direct explanation as to why we should not cut the hair at the sides of our head or clip our beards. While many of the laws in the Torah seem self-evidently sensible rules around which to organise a society, some seem frankly bizarre.

Deuteronomy 25:11–12 tells us that if two men are fighting and the wife of one of them grabs his opponent by the testicles, you should cut her hand off. No explanation. Exodus 23:19 tells us we must not boil a baby goat in the milk of its mother. We are left to deduce for ourselves the logic behind this law. Leviticus 22:24 tells us that we must not make sacrifices to God of animals whose testicles are bruised or otherwise damaged. How we can tell if our animals' testicles are bruised, or why God does not like such sacrifices, we can only wonder.

Nevertheless, scholars and historians say that there are usually reasons for these strange laws. It is often the case, for example, that traditional practices from neighbouring pagan religions are being prohibited. When memory of the pagan custom is lost, as is the case for modern readers, the laws seem bizarre. It may, however, have made perfect sense to the original reader, who would have understood that they were being told not to compromise their religion by incorporating the practices of other religions. This is possibly the case for boiling a kid in its mother's milk. And so we must work hard to figure out why God's divine law specifies that we must not shave. The most likely reason is that beards were a mark of distinction.

Beards of distinction

It is possible that there is some practical element to the instruction on shaving. Some have speculated that a nomadic people could be better served in terms of hygiene by avoiding shaving and by keeping their beards well oiled. (Believe it or not, there is instruction in the Bible around what to do in the event of an infection in the beard.[3]) This seems rather speculative, though, as there is little evidence that ancient peoples were troubled either by shaving or by wearing beards. There is a more obvious reason.

One central theme of the Hebrew Scriptures, and one of the biggest concerns through the story of the Old Testament, is the attempts that God made to keep his people, the Jews, separate and holy. The Jews were told time and again to keep the law that Moses had given them and to avoid adopting the

---

[3] Leviticus 13:30. I'm afraid the answer is that a priest has to check it and will declare you ritually unclean until it gets better.

customs, particularly the religious customs, of the other civil-isations with whom they came into contact.

Time and time again, the Bible tells us about times the Hebrew people adopted foreign customs and ended up worshipping foreign gods. Now, if I were to tell you that most of the Mesopotamian societies at the time the Torah was composed insisted that their priests shave, how would you suppose the Jewish people might have responded? Or if I told you that Egyptian priests shaved all their hair off and even plucked out their eyelashes to ensure they had absolutely no hair, would you spot a pattern?

The prohibitions on shaving, alongside other instructions on haircuts and clothing requirements, were largely there to ensure that the Jews kept themselves distinct and separate from the pagan faiths that surrounded and threatened them. Pagan priests shaved, so Jews should be bearded.

Beards of purity

The requirement for priests in particular not to shave comes with some extra context. There were a lot of things priests could not do. In Jewish worship, the priests were the ones who mediated between God and humans. The high priest was the only one allowed into the Holy of Holies in the Temple and his job was to make peace with God on behalf of his people and make right the sins of the nation. To do that he had to go through extensive purification rituals and sacrifices to ensure that he himself would be pure and accept-able to God before entering. That meant a number of things. He had to be 'unblemished' as an individual – morally, spir-itually and physically. He could not cut his body, marry a prostitute, tear his clothes or approach the high altar with a crippled foot or hand, an eye defect, running sores or damaged testicles.[4] The logic was that he needed to be holy before God, as God himself is holy. And the list included an instruction not to shave or leave his hair unkempt. The beard was part of the natural order of a man's face. God put it there because God wanted it there. To cut it was to mar God's creation.

Beautiful beards

In many cultures, what starts as function quickly becomes fashion. It appears that this is also the case with the Jews of Jesus' day. The beard was required under the law, but it also became the mark of a man. It became a matter of pride to have a big, bushy beard.

The Talmud is a collection of rabbinic sayings, many of which are based on interpretations of the Torah which form the basis of traditional Jewish interpretation of the Scriptures. According to the Talmud, the beard is *hadrat panim*, the glory of one's face. One passage in the Bava Metzia describes a list of beautiful men who follow on from Adam, the first man. The list includes Abraham, Isaac and Jacob and biblical patriarchs. The idea is that they followed the ideal image of man by resembling Adam. There is a notable exception, however. The sage Rabbi Yochanan was left out of this list, despite being known as a beautiful man. And the reason given is that he did not have a beard, so he could not have the kind of beauty that followed from the first man.

---

[4] Why damaged testicles should be such a source of fascination for the Old Testament writers is a topic for research this author has not yet undertaken. Deuteronomy 23:1 tells us that a man with damaged testicles or who has had their penis cut off cannot enter the assembly of the Lord. As if he hasn't suffered enough.

The story tells us more than simply that the sages who contributed to the Talmud considered the beard attractive. It shows that they considered it natural, given by God to the first man, who was handmade by God. So what we already have here is a union of religious obedience, cultural significance and fashion.

Before we leave the topic of the Bible completely, however, we should pause to consider what the New Testament has to say on the subject. The survey will not take long, as the New Testament says precisely nothing about beards. However, St Paul did have something to say about hair, which will set the scene for later theologians' views on facial hair. In his letter to the newly founded church in Corinth, Paul wrote:

> Judge for yourselves: is it proper for a woman to pray to God with her head uncovered? Does not the very nature of things teach you that if a man has long hair, it is a disgrace to him, but that if a woman has long hair, it is her glory? For long hair is given to her as a covering. If anyone wants to be contentious about this, we have no other practice – nor do the churches of God. (1 Corinthians 11:13–16)

This is a fascinating text and part of Paul's highly controversial writings about the role of women in the Church. Many today have used Paul's writings here and elsewhere to argue that men should be in charge. Paul's argument here that long hair is disgraceful to men but glorious on women may seem to be a mere statement of fashion, but it sits in a wider line of argument that the role of women is set out in nature as part of God's created order. The argument goes that God made men and women different in a number of ways and had different roles in place for them in His world. One of these ways was to make sure men were in charge.

The specific requirement for women to cover their heads in church remained in force in England until the Archbishops of

Canterbury and York issued a proclamation in 1942 that women no longer needed to wear a hat in church. The change was made in part at the request of the Board of Trade, who were concerned about wartime shortages of clothing. Other churches retained the requirement much further into the twentieth century.

Naturally, this interpretation of Paul's writings has been challenged, and it seems more likely that Paul was simply telling the church not to act outrageously or offensively within the cultural norms of the society of his day. Since it was the custom for men to have short hair, they should follow that custom, and women should follow the custom for them too. Nevertheless, we will see later how this kind of thinking was used to argue for big, manly biblical beards.

The shave that led to a war

In 2 Samuel 10, there is a fascinating story involving King David. The neighbouring king (of the Ammonites) had died and David sent envoys to the king's son and successor to express sympathies. This went down badly, however, as they thought it odd that David did not come himself and speculated that the envoys may be spies on a scouting mission. So, in response, they cut the backside out of their trousers and shaved half their beards.

The message was sent back to David that his men had been humiliated in this way, so he said to them, 'Stay at Jericho till your beards have grown, and then come back' (verse 5). No guidance was given on what to do with their trousers.

But the Ammonites then realised they had angered King David with this action, so they hired a large number of mercenaries. David heard about this, and the whole incident escalated into full-scale war between them. The Bible records that King David killed 700 of their charioteers and 40,000 of their foot soldiers.

If there is a moral to this story, it will be for others to work it out. But we can see that the beard had such an important place in Jewish culture, that forcibly shaving an enemy was the height of humiliation. It was a matter of obedience to God to let it grow and a matter of personal purity to keep God's creation long and lustrous. It was a matter of great pride – and a matter of great humiliation to be forcefully shaved.

2

A Multitude of Chins: Holy Beards

The Bible says that love covers a multitude of sins. Over the years, the love of Jesus has led to the covering of a multitude of chins. Some of the most important theologians in the history of Christianity have, astoundingly to us, considered questions like, 'What are men's nipples for?'; 'Is it natural to have a beard or to learn to shave it off?'; and, 'What do hairy chests signify?' But why?

As we answer these questions it will be hard to ignore the implications for other areas of biblical study and theology. It is clear that the cultural milieu of the theologians of the past influenced their views on beards so we are left to wonder in what other ways the church fathers were influenced by the cultures in which they lived. Theological ideas around the significance of facial hair developed in the same way and from the same people as many of Christianity's most important doctrines. Sometimes these came about through the study of Scripture, but often the development of theology started with the assumptions implicit in the culture of the day. Scripture and reason were applied with a set of presuppositions around gender roles in place before Scripture could be interpreted. We have been living with the impact of these norms and expectations of gender roles ever since.

Imitators of Christ's facial hair

If we take a brief sojourn back to the very start of this tale, the narrator of the energetic and insightful work you are reading with such great interest asked how confident we can be that Jesus had a beard. I hope it has now been demonstrated that we can be as sure as we can be on any historical fact that Jesus definitely had one. He simply would not have been an Orthodox Jew of his time if he had not grown as big and bushy a beard as nature permitted.

Nevertheless, as soon as Christianity travelled outside the Orthodox Jewish community, the nature of Christ's facial hair became a matter of debate. That left plenty of room for his followers to argue over whether to shave, trim or leave the beard totally untouched by human hands. And when I say argue, I mean argue. In the biblical sense.[1]

Jesus' disciples' beards

In the Jewish tradition, disciples followed their rabbi (teacher) as closely as possible in every aspect of life. When the rabbi woke, his disciples woke. When the rabbi ate, his disciples ate. When the rabbi prayed, his disciples prayed. There is no question that Jesus' disciples would have been bearded, just as their Lord was. Nevertheless, the tradition of the Church does not always present them as such.

Da Vinci's *The Last Supper* is a classic depiction of Christ with his disciples. It shows their reactions when they heard Jesus tell them he would be betrayed. It is unquestionably a

---

[1] The biblical sense of arguing is to argue a lot and very forcefully, leading to all-out war if the protagonists feel necessary or are simply unable to stop themselves.

masterpiece and uses traditional depictions of the disciples from Western art.

The painting was completed in 1498, though it was not until the nineteenth century that one of Da Vinci's notebooks was found, revealing the name of each of the disciples. It has become possibly the most famous representation of all the disciples together. A number of them are shown clean shaven. Perhaps most notably, John looks positively boy-like in his complexion. Philip and Matthew are clean shaven and the rest have short, trimmed beards. As we have seen before, this is a recreation of history in our own image; Da Vinci painted them all with pale skin and European appearance.

THE LAST SUPPER
BEARD DETAILS

BARTHOLOMEW* JAMES* ANDREW* THOMAS* JAMES* PHILIP

JESUS*

JUDAS* PETER* JOHN MATTHEW JUDE* SIMON*

* – BEARDED

The presentation of the disciples with and without beards varies between different pieces of art, although there is some commonality in the convention. Those disciples considered to have been older have beards, and the younger ones do not. The Bible does not mention the ages of the disciples. However, church tradition has suggested that John was the last-surviving disciple, who died in the last decade of the first century, so is often considered to have been the youngest. Peter is sometimes considered the oldest, as the Bible mentions that he was already married when he began to follow Jesus.

Early church teaching: the first five hundred years of beard theology

In the fourth century AD, in what is now known as Algeria, there was a Roman outpost called Thagaste. Not notable for any commercial or cultural significance, it was a perfectly ordinary North African town. There, a lady called Monica married Patricius, a humble, free man. They were Berbers, the indigenous ethnic group in North Africa, but were heavily Romanised. They spoke Latin and followed the traditional pagan religion of the Roman Empire until Monica converted to Christianity.

Monica had a difficult life. She bore two sons and probably several daughters. One day she had a dream that her sons would become Christians.

Her dream came true in AD 386, when one of her sons, Aurelius Augustinus, became a Christian at the age of 31. He heard a voice telling him, 'Take up and read,' which he understood as a divine instruction to read the Bible. He would become Bishop of Hippo in AD 395, where he remained until his death in AD 430. During that time, he became arguably the most influential theologian in the history of Christendom, besides the apostles and Jesus himself. He is simply known now as Augustine. Or Augustine of Hippo. Or St Augustine. Or Big Gus.[2]

Augustine shaped many of the Church's beliefs and spent much of his adult life fighting against heresies that were

---

[2] OK, that one is just me.

gaining traction in the early church. Augustine was, however, heavily influenced by the Greek philosophers who had gone before him. It is often argued that Augustine effectively merged the Platonic philosophy of the classical world with Christian theology to produce the teaching in the Church that we recognise today.

Plato taught that you could discern what was good by observing nature and working out what nature inclined towards. When it came to people, we could use the common sense we were born with to work out human virtues by observing what nature intended. This became known as natural law. Augustine believed that, since God had made the world, this was a fair approach to take. The only difference was that he concluded it was the intention of God the creator, rather than nature, that could be revealed by this examination.

Fortunately for the sake of the narrative contained within these pages, both had something to say about beards. They loved them, in fact. Augustine, along with almost all the major early church fathers, argued that the beard was essential for Christians.

Beard theology

The story of what the early Christians decided with regard to beards, and how they decided it, tells us a lot about how they formed their views on just about everything theological. The Catholic and Anglican denominations consider three sources of authority for working out theological issues: the Bible, tradition and reason. Reformed protestants will argue for just one: the Bible. *Sola Scriptura* (Scripture alone) was one of the rallying cries of the Reformation. You might imagine that arguments for or against wearing a beard might come from one of these three perspectives. You might expect to see arguments related to Scripture or historic church teachings. But you would be wrong.

The first arguments made by the major early church fathers, who shaped the theology the Church holds right up to this day, were based on natural law. As we have seen, this involved looking at what existed in nature and trying to work out God's intentions and will from it.

The trouble with this method is that it was predicated on the way the church fathers perceived nature. Their basic assumptions about the world around them were defined by the culture of the day and by the classical scientific theories of Hippocrates, Aristotle and Plato.[3] As a result, cultural norms and classical philosophy were interpreted as a form of divine plan for humanity.

Within this context, the beard was given due consideration by Augustine:

> There are some details of the body which are there for simply aesthetic reasons, and for no practical purpose – for instance, the nipples on a man's chest, and the beard on his face, the latter being clearly for a masculine ornament, not for protection. This is shown by the fact that women's faces are hairless, and since women are the weaker sex, it would surely be more appropriate for them to be given such a protection.[4]

We must pause momentarily to note the observation that a man's nipples were put in their place by our maker for

---

[3] More on Hippocrates' contribution to the history of beards will follow, but you will just have to wait for that.

[4] Augustine of Hippo, *City of God*, book 22, c. AD 410.

'aesthetic reasons', but we will move on swiftly.[5] Augustine's reasoning on this matter was influenced by culturally inherited views on gender roles, rather than on a strict reading of the biblical texts. He argued that a man's beard was created by God as a 'masculine ornament', because the only other possible explanation for its existence would be that a bushy beard could form a protective barrier from facial injuries. However, since women were not given the benefit of such protection, that cannot possibly be the reason.

While there is a certain logic to the argument,[6] the fallacy rests in Augustine missing the possibility of another explanation entirely for the existence of beards. It is odd that he felt the need to refute the idea that beards were a form of protection, indicating that, if there were any other possibilities in his mind, they too would have been addressed.

Augustine, alongside other early church fathers, argued that it was beneficial to show the manliness of the beard grower and therefore their distinctiveness from women, who were not blessed with such things.

Psalm 133 begins, 'How good and pleasant it is when God's people live together in unity! It is like precious oil poured on the head, running down on the beard, running down on Aaron's beard, down on the collar of his robe.'

Augustine wrote a commentary on this psalm, in which he wrote, 'To the beard. The beard signifies the courageous; the

---

[5] We can hardly blame them for not knowing that males and females both develop from the same genetic blueprint in the womb and develop nipples before the Y chromosome begins developing testes for male foetuses at six or seven weeks into the pregnancy.

[6] Your author would be the first to acknowledge that it is one of the weakest arguments that Augustine has ever made, but is merely accepting that there is a tiny element of logic buried within it.

beard distinguishes the grown men, the earnest, the active, the vigorous. So that when we describe such, we say, he is a bearded man.'[7]

Again, Augustine is not making his argument directly from the Bible. He is attempting to explain what he reads in the Bible using his reading of nature, based on the cultural norms he has inherited about the world around him. To the modern reader, it is clear that he is reading much of the cultural context of his day into this. The beard may well have signified courageousness in Augustine's time, but to different people in different ages the beard could just as easily signify the barbarian, the vagabond or the hipster. Beards do not have an inherent positive or negative sentiment.

This way of doing theology has played its part in many other debates on some of the most contentious topics in the Church. Gender roles were assumed or, at best, divined from nature (by men). Men were not just different from women, but also considered to be superior physically, spiritually and morally. The beard was simply a symbol of this.

Even more beard theology

Augustine's observations about the natural order of men and women were not the only arguments used in favour of the beard among these early church fathers.

Before Augustine came Clement of Alexandria, born in AD 150. He converted to Christianity as an adult and became a teacher of theology in a school for priests and theologians in Egypt. His works show that he was very familiar with classical Greek philosophy, and his theology was influenced by philosophers such as Plato and the Stoics.

---

[7] Augustine, *Exposition on Psalm 133*, 6.

And Clement had a lot to say about body hair.

Clement's *The Instructor* was made up of three books, one of which contained the chapter, 'Against men who embellish themselves'. The majority of the chapter is an argument that men should let nature take its course with their facial and body hair:

> *How womanly it is for one who is a man to comb himself and shave himself with a razor, for the sake of fine effect, and to arrange his hair at the mirror, shave his cheeks, pluck hairs out of them, and smooth them . . . for God wished women to be smooth and to rejoice in their locks alone growing spontaneously, as a horse in his mane. But he adorned man like lions, with a beard, and endowed him as an attribute of manhood, with a hairy chest – a sign of strength and rule . . .*
>
> *It is therefore impious to desecrate the symbol of manhood, hairiness.*[8]

This baffling piece of man-theology argues that God is delighted that women pluck, shave and wax their way to smooth skin, but is happiest when men are hairy. Why the Lord would not be pleased with a woman who lets nature take its course on her hairy places is not explained, nor why male smoothness is so displeasing to our maker.

We should note that when Clement says, 'How womanly', this is not intended as a favourable reference to the female gender. Womanly was, to Clement, inferior to manly. He believed men to be stronger not just physically, but in every respect. The hairy chest of a man was not just a quirk of our biology, but a sign of strength and rule. What is more, these things were not matters that had to be deduced by careful study of the evidence, but simple and self-evident

---

[8] Clement of Alexandria, *The Instructor*, 3, III.

facts that presented themselves through nature. As far as Clement was concerned, it is not our place to consider or alter the aesthetics of our own faces. It is our responsibility to live with the facial hair that the Lord created in his divine providence. To shave, cut, trim or style your facial hair is to presume to know better than our maker how we should be presented.

Of course, some have noted that the Lord also inspired man to make five-blade safety razors, easy-glide shaving gel and age-defying moisturising cream, so where does that leave us?

Fortunately for students of church history, there is more to the ancient theological debate on beards than simply an emphasis on gender division.

REASONS FOR HAVING A BEARD

TO DEMONSTRATE MANLINESS
AND THAT KIND OF THING

SHAVING IS A BIT TOO
MUCH OF A BOTHER,
IF TRUTH BE TOLD

A CUNNING DISGUISE

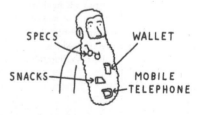

STORAGE SPACE
FOR SUNDRY ITEMS

Notable quotables

We must now avoid the trap of trawling through the writings of all the early church fathers for any mention of beards. I have tried it and I can assure you that there are better ways to spend your weekends. However, there are a few notable quotes that merit a mention:

Church father	Who was he?	Beard theology
Tertullian (AD 160–220).	Another North African who was a prolific writer at the end of the second and start of the third century AD. He was the first to use the word 'Trinity' to describe the three persons of God.	'Nor may men destroy the hair of their beards, and unnaturally change the form of a man. For the law says: "Ye shall not mar your beards." For God the Creator has made this decent for women, but has determined that it is unsuitable for men. But if thou do these things to please men, in contradiction to the law, thou wilt be abominable with God, who created thee after His own image. If, therefore, thou wilt be acceptable to God, abstain from all those things which He hates, and do none of those things that are unpleasing to Him.'
Cyprian (AD 210–258)	A controversial figure when he rose to the position of Bishop of Carthage in North Africa soon after his conversion to Christianity and baptism. He held firm in the face of heresy and was eventually martyred, which sealed his reputation.	'Do we believe that a man is lamenting with his whole heart, that he is entreating the Lord with fasting, and with weeping, and with mourning, who from the first day of his sin daily frequents the bathing-places with women who, feeding at rich banquets, and puffed out with fuller dainties, belches forth on the next day his indigestions, and does not dispense of his meat and drink so as to aid the necessity of the poor? How does he who walks with joyous and glad step mourn for his death? And although it is written, "Ye shall not mar the figure of your beard," he plucks out his beard, and dresses his hair; and does he now study to please anyone who displeases God?' And: 'In their manners, there was no discipline. In men, their beards were defaced.'

| Lactantius (AD 240–329). | Like Augustine, a North African Berber. He was an influential writer and became an advisor to the Emperor Constantine, so in many ways one of the most influential Christians in history. He saw God's creative power displayed in the perfection of the human form. And so the beard is one part of God's perfect creation. And you really shouldn't mess around with something that God has already made perfect. | 'But, however, though nakedness itself on the part of man tends in a wonderful manner to beauty, yet it was not adapted to his head; for what great deformity there would be in this, is evident from baldness. Therefore, He clothed the head with hair; and because it was about to be on the top, He added it as an ornament, as it were, to the highest summit of the building. And this ornament is not collected into a circle, or rounded into the figure of a cap, lest it should be unsightly by leaving some parts bare; but it is freely poured forth in some places, and withdrawn in others, according to the comeliness of each place. Therefore, the forehead entrenched by a circumference, and the hair put forth from the temples before the ears, and the uppermost parts of these being surrounded after the manner of a crown, and all the back part of the head covered, display an appearance of wonderful comeliness. Then the nature of the beard contributes in an incredible degree to distinguish the maturity of bodies, or to the distinction of sex, or to the beauty of manliness and strength; so that it appears that the system of the whole work would not have been in agreement, if anything had been made otherwise than it is.' |

Brushing (or perhaps combing) over what Lactantius said about baldness to save the blushes of any follicly challenged readers, we can see here that Lactantius is making his argument not from Scripture or traditional church teaching, but from an interpretation of nature. He is ploughing the same theological field that Augustine would later cultivate.

Cyprian made an argument from Scripture as well as from nature, which summed up what we have seen from the other church fathers. From nature they could see that men were self-evidently superior to women and so men's beards must be a divine sign of their superiority. This was confirmed to them when they saw the Leviticus text not to 'mar the edges of your beard'. Some also saw the Jewish tradition, from which Jesus emerged, and concluded that this validated their beliefs. If we are generous, that meant that they could conclude based on Scripture, tradition and reason that God wanted his menfolk hairy-faced. That would be the very height of generosity, however. While some may have considered that text to be obscure and challenging to interpret, when it simply confirms your expectation that God would think shaving to be a terrible thing to do, the text makes perfect sense.

The beginning of beard heresy

So the early church was a bearded church. Its adherents wore their beards with pride. If the remaining images of Euthymius the Great are anything to go by, his was one of the mightiest beards in Christendom, flowing down well past his waist.

Euthymius lived between AD 377 and 473 in Palestine. He withdrew to live the life of a hermit in a cave. Annoyingly for someone pursuing the hermit's life, he began to attract followers, and so his rough cave became a church and a monastery. After he miraculously healed the son of a Saracen chief, his solitary days were well and truly over. Large crowds came to visit him in his cave monastery, so he ran away and withdrew again to the wilderness near the Dead Sea. After attracting more followers there, he made his final escape to the desert of Zipho, south of Hebron in Judea. It is hard to get some peace sometimes.

In his early days, as he established his cave monastery, he introduced the rule that only men with beards could join. He was not much of a diplomat, and he actually declared that he would not accept boys 'with female faces'.

So far, so normal. That is exactly what we would expect. Early Christian with a big beard and a theological persuasion that related beards to masculinity and God's design for male superiority. However, a few short years afterwards, we find that the Church was not at all united on this critical question. In truth, it was not united on many questions at all, but the most visible of them was the division over beards. In the end, it led to the total split of the Church between East and West into the Latin Church, based in Rome and the Eastern Orthodox Church, based in Constantinople.

In AD 286, Augustus divided the Roman Empire into two. Emperors had been struggling with the logistical challenges of governing an empire of such great size, and Augustus came up with the idea of simply splitting it into two. The Western Empire included the provinces of North Africa up to Hadrian's Wall in the north of England, including modern Spain, France, Germany, Italy and much of Eastern Europe. The Eastern Empire was the remainder of the territory from Macedonia to the Middle East. This half would outlast the Western Empire and would eventually become the Byzantine Empire. In AD 476, the Western Roman Empire fell.

Emperor Constantine the Great moved his residence to the previously small Greek town of Byzantium in AD 330. He renamed it Nova Roma. Constantine was the first Roman emperor to convert to Christianity, and his move to decriminalise and eventually promote Christianity was the turning point for the new religion in the Empire.

In the earliest days of Christianity there was really only one Church. We see in the letters of Paul in the Bible a desire to keep tabs on the new churches he founded and to keep their increasingly dodgy theology and practices in order. As the Church grew, this would prove to be a task even greater than that faced by the Roman emperors seeking to maintain order across their Empire. Just as the Roman Empire facilitated the spread of Christianity, so the division of the Roman Empire resulted in a split in the Church.

In the years that followed, the decline of the Western Roman Empire and the strength of the Byzantine Empire led to a power struggle between the two religious centres – Rome and Constantinople. Both claimed to be the centre of Christianity, Rome through a line of continuity of its bishops from St Peter, and Constantinople through its position in the world as the global centre of Christendom. Both the Bishop of Rome – the Pope – and the Patriarch of Constantinople claimed primacy within the Church until they eventually excommunicated each other. Canon 3 of the First Council of Constantinople in AD 381 stated that the Bishop of that city 'shall have primacy of honour after the Bishop of Rome because Constantinople is the New Rome'. Soon he would claim authority even over the

BEARDS IN RELIGIOUS FESTIVALS

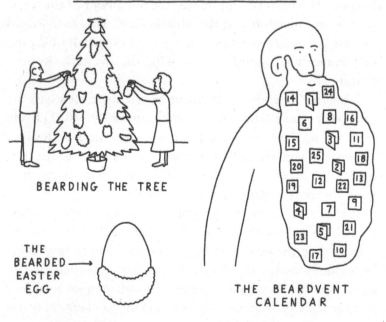

BEARDING THE TREE

THE
BEARDED ——→
EASTER
EGG

THE BEARDVENT
CALENDAR

Bishop of Rome. Two factions formed in the Church, and we see the emergence of the Latin Church of the West and the Orthodox Church of the East.

Our narrative will return to this topic in due course, but for the meantime it is sufficient to note that the Eastern Church did not trouble itself with too much consideration of the topic of facial hair. It was happy to live with the theology passed down from the early church fathers and was very much a bearded Church. This suited it well, being a bearded Church within a bearded society. There was no social or cultural conflict. There was no theological conflict.

However, over on the Western side of the Church, a largely clean-shaven Roman society was very much at odds with the bearded Church that had evolved. And so the Church found reasons to make its peace with the razor blade. And once it had done so, it not only accepted shaving, but it also mandated it, and in some cases even threatened excommunication to those who disobeyed these important rules.

PART II
SHAVING FOR THE GODS

3

In the Beginning was the Beard

Since the dawn of time men have shaved and have done so in order to please their gods. Remarkably, among the earliest evidence of human development and civilisation is evidence of hair removal. The first civilisations on earth all had a special place either for the beard or for shaving.

These stories are a source of historical interest for the religious history of facial hair in their own right. But they are also the societies from within which the Hebrew culture emerged. If we want to understand the place of beards in the Jewish and Christian traditions, the story begins much further back. Let us delve as far back as recorded history allows, to find the beginning of the story.

History's first shavers

One of the most pivotal moments in the history of humankind was the moment around ten thousand years ago when someone had a bright idea. Rather than wander around looking for animals to hunt and crops to gather, people realised they could stay in one place, grow their own crops and raise animals. For reasons we cannot explain, this bright idea seems to have been had by quite a few people round the world at almost exactly the same time. 'Let's become an agrarian society,' they said to each other. And they did.

One such place was Mesopotamia.

From within these permanent settlements, the age of stone gave way to bronze, and the first genuine civilisation grew up in Sumer in Southern Mesopotamia, modern-day Iraq. Uruk in Sumer is believed to have been the first city in the history of humankind. Historians believe that a permanent settlement began there between 5500 and 4000 BC, and a clear historical record commenced around 3000 BC with the invention of writing.

For this reason, the region is known today as the 'cradle of civilisation'. It is also the region from which Judaism emerged, in turn giving birth to Christianity and Islam. So, for the purposes of our story, it is well worth a brief dip into the cool and refreshing waters of the place to which most of the world's great religions trace their origin, and where beard theology begins.

The earliest archaeological finds in this region are the kinds of things we would expect to find in an ancient civilisation: building foundations, clay pots, tools, TripAdvisor reviews of the local copper dealers[1] and, of course, razors and shaving paraphernalia. Copper razors have been found, dating from the earliest period of civilisation in Mesopotamia.

SHAVING
DEVELOPMENT OVER TIME

 → → (ETC)

STONE FLINT   TWIN-BLADE   TRIPLE-BLADE
                     STONE FLINT   STONE FLINT

---

[1] One clay tablet found in the Sumerian city of Ur dating from around 1750 BC is a complaint from someone called Nanni to his copper dealer accusing him of giving his slave 'ingots that were not good'. The ancient equivalent of a bad TripAdvisor review.

In a sense, our story begins here. The earliest historical record of civilised Homo Sapiens shows that they shaved. In fact, they not only shaved, but also plucked and even waxed.[2] In almost all civilisations, archaeologists have found evidence of hair-removal devices. Based on evidence from early cave paintings, some believe that this began as early as a hundred thousand years ago. Such evidence is rather sketchy, though.[3]

We cannot know why those earliest people took such an interest in hair removal. But in the case of our Mesopotamian friends, we do know that they shaved for a particular reason: to keep the gods happy.

~

The gods were a rather important feature in the life of the average Mesopotamian in 3000 BC. Besides letters of complaint, the earliest forms of writing tell stories of the gods making order from chaos, creating the world and giving birth to the Sumerian people. They tell epic tales of a great flood where humankind was saved by the building of an ark.[4] The Epic of Gilgamesh, the part-human, part-divine King of Uruk, dates from Sumer around 2000 BC. The rich archaeological evidence from this period has left behind a wealth of information on the lives and beliefs of the Sumerian people, and it is obvious that pleasing the gods was a major part of their lives.

One of the great Sumerian kings was Shulgi. He reigned between 2094 and 2047 BC. Shulgi's greatest love was, well, Shulgi.

---

[2] We know that the Egyptians 'waxed' using a mixture of sugar and water applied to linen strips.

[3] Cave paintings . . . sketchy . . . geddit?!

[4] One version of this story from Sumer dating from around 1900 BC even names Noah as the central character who collected animals in an ark to protect them from a great flood.

Ancient Spa and Hair Removal Menu

Here at the Ancient Spa and Hair Removal Clinic, we
use only authentic ancient methods of making sure
your face is acceptable and pleasing to the gods by
getting rid of all your unholy hair.

1. Pumice facial scrub
*Our most affordable treatment. Bring out your stone-
age chic by rubbing away unwanted hair with volcanic
stone. Not ideal for those with sensitive skin.*

2. Clam shell tweezer pluck
*Almost as ancient as the pumice facial scrub, the clam shell
pluck is a lot less painful! A good choice for those who
aren't that bothered how much hair gets removed, since
clam shells are not the most effective form of tweezers.*

3. Stone flint shave
*Our entry-level shave, we use a sharpened flint blade to
shave those unwanted hairs. Be sure to ask for plenty of
soothing cold water on your face after this stone-age treat.*

4. Bronze razor shave and wax
*Walk like an Egyptian and step into the Bronze Age
with this mid-level shaving experience. It comes with a
luxury shaving cream made by extracting alkali from
wood and mixing it with animal fat to apply to the
beard before shaving. Any remaining hair will be
removed by applying linen strips coated with sugar and
water to the body, then pulling them away when the
mixture has hardened.*

5. Copper razor shave

Shave like a Roman with a novacila *(copper razor).
You'll look as sharp as a centurion and your razor is
guaranteed to stay sharp through your whole shave
(unlike those soft bronze razors). We'll start with a
shave, then rub down with pumice any stubble that's
left, before soothing your skin with massage oils and
perfume in an authentic Roman barber shop experience. No need to worry about shaving cuts either. Any
nicks are treated with thick ointment made from spider
webs soaked in oil and vinegar. Pure luxury.*

Shulgi wrote a poem in praise of himself which opens
with the typically humble line, 'I, the king, was a hero
already in the womb.' It goes on to describe a man of near
superhuman abilities (or actual superhuman abilities in
many instances) in almost every aspect of life. Near the end
of the first verse he reassuringly tells us, 'Truly I am not
boasting!'

As a great king in a great civilisation, Shulgi has left us
more than his fair share of the archaeological record in the
form of writings, paintings and sculptures. This means that
we know quite a bit about him and his life. This evidence
points to two key issues that drove Shulgi.

Like all ancient peoples, the Sumerians lived their lives in
fear of two great threats: the wrath of the gods and enemy
invaders. The job of the king was to appease the gods and
repel the enemy. The king needed to be a great warrior capable
of leading his armies into battle and instilling fear in his
enemies, while also making sure the gods were happy enough
with the people to send rain, grow crops and keep away
disease. Shulgi's poem is designed to describe these two
aspects of his character: his strength and his piety.

He took these duties seriously. In his self-promotion song, Shulgi describes how he once honoured the gods in Nippur in the morning, ran a hundred miles on foot to the city of Ur to make sacrifices to Nanna, the moon god, then nipped straight back to Nippur to repeat his sacrifices there.

Bronze statuettes have been found in Shulgi's home town of Ur, his capital and a holy city, of the king fulfilling his priestly duties. They are a stylised form of a man carrying offerings to the gods in a basket on his head.

In other representations we see Shulgi the warrior king, looking every bit the lion he compares himself with in his own promotional literature. In rock carvings from the same period we see him holding his weapons of bow and sword while trampling his enemies underfoot.

Besides the differing contexts for these two images, there is another striking difference. When Shulgi is represented as the priest-king he is clean shaven. Shulgi the warrior-king, however, has a long, impressive, flowing beard.

Some have speculated that the king would shave for important religious festivals, while others believe that both the long beard and the clean-shaven look are exaggerations for PR purposes, but whatever the explanation, the intent of the imagery is the same. The gods demanded purity, and shaving was an important part of that, while tough, macho warriors were bearded.

Shaving for purity has obvious advantages. Mesopotamia was hot. In an age where male grooming products could hardly even be described as rudimentary, beards could get smelly, unkempt and lice-ridden. Not the sort of thing that makes a good impression on a discerning pagan god.

The warrior, however, needs to show that he has reached full strength and maturity. He needs to be able to intimidate the enemy with a fierce appearance. And the big beard does just that.

The real champions of the beard in ancient Mesopotamia had to be the Assyrians. In their art and sculpture they are depicted with long, neatly curled beards. Their literature describes well-oiled beards, decorated with ribbons and charms. Rather delightful. Or possibly terrifying, which was more the intended impact.

Assyria was ruled by Sumer from around 2500 BC, so shared many of its cultural trappings. The Assyrians seem to have been more keen on being warriors than being pious, however, so took their love of beards further than their neighbours.

This was continued by the Babylonians as their civilisation rose to dominate the region from around 1900 BC. They retained the tradition of shaving before the gods, but only for priests from the time of their consecration. Everybody else concentrated on war more than on worship. Babylonian art always shows men with long, neatly curled beards.

In Babylon, the full beard had become something of an art form. There was, however, one ancient civilisation that uniquely revered the goatee.

The holy goatee of eternal life

If you ask someone to think about ancient Egypt, one of the first images that will come to mind is the golden death mask of King Tut – or, as he is sometimes known, Tutankhamun. This is a beautiful realistic impression of the teenage king when he died, now housed in the Egyptian Museum in Cairo. You can see his full lips and his broad cheekbones. He is presented in the traditional ceremonial headdress and long goatee beard. The only odd thing about it is that he died as a teenager, well before he could have grown a long beard.

Walk round the Metropolitan Museum of Art in New York and you will find another iconic image from ancient Egypt.

Standing more than a metre and a half tall in pink granite is a sphynx. Exquisitely carved, the muscular torso of a lion combines with the face of the Pharaoh Hatshepsut, wearing the traditional Pharaoh's ceremonial headdress and osird – the divine goatee beard.

Hatshepsut was the fifth Pharaoh of the Eighteenth Dynasty of Egypt and became Pharaoh in 1507 BC. The reign of Hatshepsut marked a minor renaissance in the Egyptian civilisation. Hatshepsut established trade routes, which brought new prosperity to Egypt after a period of relative decline, and was a prolific builder. Statues and monuments from this period are in virtually every major collection of Egyptian artefacts held today.

Hatshepsut's memorial temple at Deir el-Bahri was considered one of the architectural wonders of ancient Egypt. From that period onwards, Egypt's civilisation prospered, leading to the reign of Ramesses the Great around 250 years later. In other words, Hatshepsut was a pretty big deal.[5]

Hatshepsut was also a woman. It would be a further 1400 years before Cleopatra would become eternally renowned as Egypt's most famous female Pharaoh. But Hatshepsut paved the way, and her rule was quite unprecedented for a female ruler anywhere on earth (as far as we know). She reigned as a divine ruler for two decades and left a lasting legacy.

Like all Pharaohs, Hatshepsut is often depicted wearing a long goatee beard. Beards were so important to a Pharaoh's image that a powerful female Pharaoh and a teenage boy

---

[5] If you are wondering why you have not heard more about this incredible female Pharaoh, one of the reasons is that her successors attempted to wipe her name from the history books by literally wiping her name from all her monuments. They very nearly succeeded, until archaeologists recently uncovered the incredible temples and monuments she built.

Pharaoh would want to be seen wearing one. This hints at the important symbolism of beards in ancient Egyptian culture and religion.

In the early years of the Egyptian civilisation, beards were commonplace. Moustaches and full beards are depicted in art and mummy masks up to the start of the Middle Kingdom, around 2000 BC. For example, carvings depicting King Narmer, who is thought to have ruled a unified kingdom in around 3150 BC, show almost all the men as bearded. This was the start of the Dynastic Period, as the collection of settlements around the Nile formed a cohesive kingdom and civilisation. From then on, shaving appears to have become more commonplace and, eventually, the norm for nobles and commoners alike. By the time of Hatshepsut's reign, only the lowest in social status or those in mourning would allow their beards to grow.

The principal reason for Egyptians shaving was probably to do with an almost obsessive quest for personal hygiene and the obvious benefit in comfort that being clean shaven would bring in a hot and humid climate. Almost all ancient Egyptians would shave not only their heads but also all their body hair. However, we often see depictions in Egyptian art of a wide variety of hairstyles, from afros to braids and plaits. These would have been wigs, designed to keep the sun off the head and the wearer cool.

Body hair, wherever it appeared, was seen as something rather unclean and ugly. The shaved civilisation of Egypt, unquestionably at this time the most advanced and prosperous in the world they knew, looked down on the barbarians around them who sported unkempt hair and beards.

For the Pharaoh, who presented him or herself as a divine ruler, the practical side of personal hygiene appealed. Becoming ill was rather a bad style for someone claiming to be a god. The clean-shaven style therefore became associated with purity. As a result, Egyptian priests were required not only to shave all their body hair, but also to pluck the hairs of their eyebrows and eyelashes. Well, quite.

Shaving also had the benefit of allowing the Pharaoh to maintain a youthful image. The Egyptians considered the prime of life for men to be just after the point when a young male becomes a man. Shaving would let the Pharaoh kid others, and himself, that he was always at that point.

So function and fashion combined to form a deeper desire for a shaved appearance as a sign of cultural superiority, cleanliness and youthful vigour. For the Pharaohs, the importance of this clean-shaven purity was so high that they would often be buried with their barber so that they could continue to receive regular shaves in the afterlife.[6]

If the ancient Egyptians considered beards unclean and barbaric, while clean-shaven heads and bodies were physically and spiritually pure, it rather begs the question why Pharaohs would be shown with a goatee beard.

By way of explanation, allow me to introduce you to Osiris.

Osiris was the god of transitions. He was the god of resurrection and regeneration. Osiris was the god who brought new life through the cycles of the natural world and the annual flooding of the Nile. He was depicted as eternally youthful, indicating his association with eternal life and regeneration.

The Book of the Dead is the Egyptian funerary text dating from around 1500 BC. It describes the rituals and spells needed to help a soul move from this world into the next and was painted in part or in full on coffins, sarcophagi and tomb walls, designed to be close to the deceased to help guide them on their journey to the afterlife. Perhaps the most famous depiction is on the north wall of Tutankhamun's tomb.

---

[6] To help them, Pharaoh and barber were often buried with jewel-encrusted, solid-gold razors, which was unlikely to have been of much consolation to the barber.

The text tells us how Egyptians viewed their reception into the afterlife after the necessary rites on earth. They would be met on arrival by the god Osiris, after an arduous journey across the sky in the arc of the sun. Osiris was a hugely important god. And he had a long goatee.

It is for this reason that Pharaohs, priests and many others imitated his facial hair. The Pharaoh wearing an Osiris imitation fake beard was a way of suggesting that they were, in fact, best mates. They would, of course, be clean shaven, but for ceremonial purposes they would don a thin, plaited false beard, made from goat hair and coated with decorative materials. For the Pharaoh, that meant gold.

The ultimate ceremony, of course, was the Pharaoh's own funeral. In the British Museum you can find an infant's coffin, the mummy case of which contains the unmistakable shape of the Osiris beard. The famous golden death mask of Tutankhamun has made the image something that is associated with ancient Egypt the world over. Even children and youngsters like the 19-year-old King Tut could wear this goatee of eternal life.

Putting on the holy goatee was a sign that the wearer could look forward to being welcomed into the afterlife and on to eternal life by their great mate Osiris.

The combination of the clean-shaven face and the false beard served a dual symbolic purpose. Pharaohs portrayed themselves as eternally youthful in their painted and carved images, not only with smooth, firm skin, but also with the Osiris beard that linked them with the god who would bring them to eternal youth in the afterlife.

The ancient civilisations of Mesopotamia and Egypt show us that beards, and the lack thereof, have been associated with fashion, function, culture and faith from the very earliest recorded times. And not much changed in the millennia that followed.

We should also pause to note that ancient Egypt marked the high point for the humble goatee. It would be many centuries before it returned into fashion in eighteenth- and nineteenth-century Britain and America, when beard innovation really took off. So we shall be saying goodbye to the goatee for now.

4

Smooth Classics: Beards in Ancient Greece and Rome

The Roman civilisation is the one into which Jesus was born. Being Jewish, his cultural context was heavily influenced by the Mesopotamians and the Egyptians as the dominant civilisations during the emergence of the Jewish religion and culture. But he was born into a Greco–Roman world, a world in which the multitude of pagan gods was believed to be ever present and constantly interfering in the lives of mortals. It will be no surprise to learn that they had something to say about beards too.

As we will see in other civilisations and contexts, the beard was more than just a fashion accessory and a religious expression; it was part of an identity. For the Romans, to be clean shaven was to possess two key identities: to be male and to be Roman. This meant that the individual who shaved was chosen by the gods for special favour. This sense of identity is why Nero threw a three-day public festival to celebrate his first shave and kept the hairs in a box dedicated to the god Jupiter.

How Alexander the Great changed the history of facial hair

The ancient Greeks, who dominated the Mediterranean from around the eighth century BC, were famously and ostentatiously bearded. The Greeks saw a large beard as a sign of masculinity, virility and wisdom. The great gods, such as Zeus and Poseidon, were mature and heavily bearded. Philosophers were bearded, and anyone who aspired to authority and statesmanship was bearded. The culture valued the beard.

Plutarch illustrated the role of beards in a story about the defence of Argos from attack by Sparta. The city was so threatened that the women took up arms alongside the men. They won the battle and marked the victory as the 'Festival of Daring', during which the women dressed as men and vice versa. The war cost the lives of many local men, however, and afterwards the women of the city found husbands from neighbouring areas. As a defiant act of self-superiority over foreign husbands, a law was passed in Argos that a bride had to wear a beard when she went to bed with her husband on their wedding night. The women of Argos wanted to show that they were just as tough as the foreign men they were marrying.

All this changed one day in 331 BC, however. The beard quickly and dramatically went out of fashion.

Alexander the Great was an exception to almost every rule. He took the throne of Macedonia at the age of 20, following the assassination of his father, Philip II. The Roman Empire was rising, but Alexander had big ideas for his own kingdom. He was tutored by Aristotle until the age of 16, which is not a bad start to your education, and Alexander was smart, strong and ambitious. He was quickly granted the generalship of the Hellenic League, the city states that made up Greece, and launched an invasion of Persia. Soon afterwards he established the world's largest empire.

Unlike his father and the other Greeks who went before him, Alexander was clean shaven. We will never know his real reasons for this. Most likely he just could not grow much of a beard and so wanted to make a virtue of being smooth chinned. Whatever the reason, the youthful Alexander looked to, and compared himself with, the demigod of Greek legend Heracles, who was youthful and beardless in the traditional representation.

As he became the great conquering general, his example alone was enough to start changing the trend, but in 331 BC Alexander struck a decisive blow against Greek beards. On the eve of what would prove to be the culmination of his conquest of Persia, he ordered his men to shave.

The story was later told by the ancient historian Plutarch that his reason was that it would make sure his men were not vulnerable to having their beards pulled when in close combat. But this appears unlikely to have been the real reason. If

BEARD-RELATED INJURIES
IN BATTLE

BEARD PULLED BY ENEMY

TRIP OVER OWN BEARD

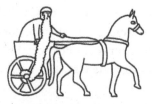

BEARD GETS CAUGHT
IN CHARIOT WHEEL

CUT SELF DURING
PRE-BATTLE GROOMING

Alexander was concerned by this, it is odd that he would wait until this moment to make the order, and no other general through history appears to have had the same concern. Much more likely, it was a form of pre-battle ritual to bind the men together and to help them stand out against the enemy.

Alexander continued to conquer new lands until he died in 323 BC. By then, his image was so widely known and his influence on the Greek culture so profound that the fashion changed completely, and beards became the preserve solely of philosophers, statesmen and wise old men.

Barba Romana

If we skip forward to 146 BC, we find ourselves surveying the scene of the Battle of Corinth. It was perhaps one of the most significant turning points in the history of western civilisation.[1] This was the final battle in the Roman conquest of Greece. After the battle, the Roman Empire came to dominate the known world, from the Atlantic Ocean to the Middle East. The form this cultural domination took was hugely influenced by the Greeks, who were defeated; the Romans adopted their religion and culture almost in its entirety. Except in one regard. By this point, Romans shaved. All of them.

Popularisation of shaving is attributed to Scipio Aemilianus, twice Consul of the Republic from 205 BC and the general who sacked Carthage in the third Punic War. Shaving became a distinction of a true Roman. Easterners and Greeks were bearded; barbarians had moustaches; Romans were clean shaven. One thing the Romans have never been short on is confidence. They knew that Romans were better than everyone else and needed

---

[1] Now be honest with yourself and confess whether you've heard of it.

little to confirm it. The fact that this small city had conquered almost the entire known world was sufficient evidence. Shaving was a way of marking out Romans for their superiority.

Shaving, for Romans, was more than just a matter of fashion, however. Romans believed that all aspects of life were in some way governed, supervised, scrutinised and regulated by a specific deity. There was a god for everything. Cardea was the Roman goddess of door hinges. With her own bizarre mythological backstory, she ruled over everything hinged.[2] Terminus was the god of mileposts, which were called 'termini' after him, and his name lives on today at the end of train lines. Sterquilinus was the god of poo and Cloacina the goddess of the sewage system in Rome. It was truly a blessed world.

Romans believed that these gods were always active in the world of mortals. Acts of injustice or hubris could invoke a response from the gods to put you back in your place. But actions pleasing to the gods could be rewarded by them with good fortune to follow.

In the Roman world, the transition from boy to man was a big moment. It was a period in history where infant mortality was probably between 20 and 30 per cent, and disease took a great toll on those who lived past childhood. Reaching adulthood was therefore a big deal, one for which it was believed the gods were largely responsible. The first growth of a beard represented for young males the elevation from youth to manhood, and the clean-shaven appearance represented the elevation of Roman civilisation above all others. Both of these were gifts from the gods and so had religious connotations.

---

[2] There were, in fact, two more gods associated with doors. Forculus was the god of double doors and Limentinus the god of thresholds. St Augustine mocked them as 'little gods' when attacking the pagan tradition of numerous deities, saying, 'Evidently Forculus can't watch the hinge and the threshold at the same time.'

THE FIRST-SHAVE PARTY

PIN THE BEARD ON THE DONKEY

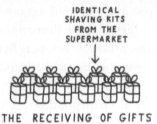

IDENTICAL SHAVING KITS FROM THE SUPERMARKET

THE RECEIVING OF GIFTS

MUSICAL BARBER'S CHAIRS

HAPPY BEARD-DAY TO YOU...

SINGING TRADITIONAL SONGS

When a freeborn Roman citizen became a man, he assumed the *toga virilis*. A sign of Roman citizenship and the uniform for all important occasions, the toga was also the standard dress for Roman priests. It carried with it religious associations – it was the dress of someone who pleased the gods.

When the first beard was ready to be shaved, the boy was ready to become a man. He would receive his toga and it would be celebrated. Often, the first hairs to be shaved would be preserved and offered to the gods. When Nero was 21 in AD 59, he went large on the celebration of his first shave. He instituted the festival of Juvenalia. Games were put on in a purpose-built theatre. He put his first beard hairs in a gold box inlaid with pearls and dedicated it to Jupiter.

The beard did not leave Rome for ever, however. The Emperor Hadrian reintroduced it to Roman society during his reign between AD 117 and 138. Dio Cassius said it was to hide his pockmarks, but it was more likely grown either out of convenience during his long campaign travels or under the influence of Greek culture, where a beard was associated with the wisdom of the philosophers. Nevertheless, beards held sway for the next 150 years or so until the Emperor Constantine appeared on the scene with an entirely smooth face. We will follow Constantine's story later in this narrative, but it should be noted that, along with the promotion of Christianity in the Roman Empire for the first time, Constantine ended the practice of growing beards in Rome for good.

While the Romans were an almost universally clean-shaven society, like those who came before and after, the beard still carried significance for their faith and to the gods.

FAKE NEWS ALERT : FAKE NEWS ALERT : FAKE NEWS

In the interests of accuracy, your humble author thought it important to address false information in the public domain in relation to the history of beards. One such item of fake news is the suggestion that the word 'barbarian' derives from the Latin barba, meaning 'bearded', and originates with Romans referring to non-Romans as those who had beards. This is a lovely story and does make sense with the history of Romans considering their clean-shaven appearance as a mark of civilised superiority. But it is completely untrue. In fact, the word 'barbarian' derives from Greek, not Roman, and has nothing to do with beards.

Barbarian
ba:'be:rien/
Noun

A person or persons not belonging to one of the great civilisations (e.g. Greek or Roman). Derives from the ancient Greek *barbaros*, which is an onomatopoeic word similar to 'gibberish' mimicking foreign languages. The Greeks referred to those who didn't speak Greek as 'barbarians', meaning people who speak like 'blah, blah, blah'.

I am afraid the fake news does not end there. Several other words have laid claim to beard-related origins. Some have claimed that the word 'bizarre' derives from the Basque word *bizaro*, meaning 'beard'. The implication is that those with beards looked odd, so it became a term of abuse. Etymologists now say that this is not true and it derives from the completely different Italian word *bizarre*, meaning 'angry'. It is often claimed that 'bigot' derives from *bigote*, meaning 'moustache' in Spanish. It does not. While *bigote* does mean 'moustache', the word 'bigot' derives from an old French word *bigot*, which means 'bigot'. It derives from sanctimonious Normans who kept swearing 'by God'.

FAKE NEWS ALERT : FAKE NEWS ALERT : FAKE NEWS

PART III
SHAVED FROM SIN: SAINTS WITH RAZORS

5

The Close Latin Shave

In the early days of the young Church, holy faces were hairy faces. We will now explore how all that changed and good Christians embraced the razor. Not only did shaving become compulsory for clerics, but the issue of clerical shaving eventually split the Church right down the middle. Between around AD 800 and 1500, the theology of beards did a complete U-turn in the Western world. While Augustine and his chums had once claimed that beards were essential to the good Christian male, we will find the devout in later times arguing that St Peter himself started the tradition of shaving in the Church.

Beard theology became weaponised amid identity politics, both between Eastern and Western Christians who disagreed on the beard and between clerics and laity in the West. The Roman Catholic Church in the West embraced clericalism and the belief that priests were specially chosen and holy, with the unique ability to mediate between people and God and to bring God's presence to earth through the sacrament of Holy Communion. And so they marked out these special people by shaving their chins and the tops of their heads.

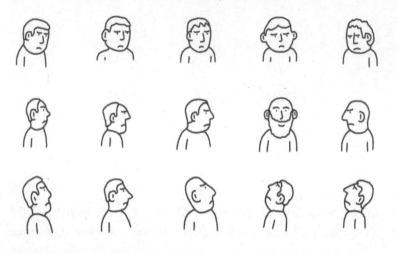

St Peter's first shave

Some have attributed the introduction of shaving to St Peter the apostle, the rock upon whom Christ built his Church. There is a long tradition within the Catholic Church of St Peter instituting the tonsure – better known today as the Friar Tuck haircut. The tonsure involved shaving the top of the head to leave just a 'crown' of hair around the outside. The origin of this tradition is somewhat unclear, but it is often attributed to St Peter.

The story starts when Peter went to Antioch, an ancient Greek city that lies in modern-day Turkey. His mission was to convert the pagans to Christianity. On arrival, however, Peter was not exactly welcomed with open arms. In fact, the pagans seized him and, in order to humiliate him, they shaved off the hair from the top of his head and his beard. Given what we know of the importance of beards to Jews (which Peter would still have considered himself), and the Old Testament story of King David's ambassadors being humiliated by having their beards shaved off, this was likely quite a serious attack.

Nevertheless, Peter was not one to rise to this sort of bait. He accepted his ordeal with humility and wore his newfound shaved face and head with pride.

In his epic 1882 essay on the history of beards in the Catholic Church, the Most Reverend Charles J. Seghers pondered, 'Is this an historical fact or a legendary tradition which may be either piously believed or discarded without harm? We shall not decide; but we could adduce such weight of testimony as would force the scales down in favour of the former alternative.' Well, this author considers this rather wishful thinking, since there is absolutely no historical evidence for any of this actually happening. But why let the facts get in the way of a good story?

Far more likely was that the new Christians in the Roman world were increasingly Gentiles who did not care one way or the other whether they had a beard, so shaved in line with the common custom of the day. They were probably encouraged to do so by the teaching of the apostle Paul, who wrote to the church in Corinth saying:

> To the Jews I became like a Jew, to win the Jews. To those under the law [Old Testament Jewish] I became like one under the law (though I myself am not under the law), so as to win those under the law. To those not having the law I became like one not having the law (though I am not free from God's law but am under Christ's law), so as to win those not having the law. To the weak I became weak, to win the weak. I have become all things to all people so that by all possible means I might save some. (1 Corinthians 9:20–2)[1]

---

[1] This letter would have been read publicly in the new early churches, then copied, passed on and spread round other new churches.

While not directly addressing the issue of shaving, it would have been understood as an encouragement to accept some of the cultural norms of the society in order to allow Christians to win acceptance and then preach the new gospel.

Beard heresy

As the Church spread rapidly through the Roman Empire, a problem emerged. Every time someone new joined the Church, they seemed to start getting Christianity wrong. The first recorded Christian theological argument is actually in the Bible, after Peter's visit to Antioch. He founded a church there, then the apostle Paul visited and found an argument raging about whether the Gentile converts to Christianity needed to be circumcised and become Jewish. Surprisingly, it seems some were reluctant. Paul argued that they didn't need to and returned to Jerusalem to call together the disciples to thrash it out. They agreed, and the entire Christian world is grateful to this day (see Acts 1–35; Galatians 2:1–21).

As the Church spread further, however, the issue of heresy grew. St Paul's letters in the Bible are full of slap-downs to young churches about their increasingly dodgy practices and, as time went on, there were no apostles left to pronounce judgement on the issues. What is more, the issues being debated were becoming more and more complicated.

By the fourth century, the problem of heresy had become so great that a solution had to be found. Among other issues, some were claiming that the Son of God had been created by God and therefore was not fully divine. Others claimed that the Son had existed from the beginning as one part of the Holy Trinity and wanted to stamp out the growing heresy known as Arianism. The great and the good of the early church came together to work the issue out in what became known as the first Ecumenical Council at Nicaea. This council gave birth to the Nicene Creed, which is still used in the Church today as one of the foundations of the Christian faith. But without a clearly defined doctrine or set of church laws, heresy proved hard to put down. It seemed that every heresy had an equal and opposite ecumenical council to try to quash it.

Councils were held regularly for the next half century in attempts to resolve debates in the Church. The biggest issues of the day and the core beliefs of orthodox Christianity were settled and established in these meetings. They also talked about beards. A lot. No fewer than seven such councils addressed the issue of shaving between the fifth and twelfth centuries, and more revisited it later. It was almost an obsession.

THE ECUMENICAL COUNCIL

- APOLOGIES
- MINUTES OF LAST ECUMENICAL COUNCIL
- ON TO ITEM ONE ON THE AGENDA:
  'WHAT IS OUR BEARD POLICY?'

The practice of clerical shaving spread rapidly and reached the furthest outpost of Western Christianity, England, by at least the seventh century. The Law of Wihtred from around AD 695 refers to priests as a 'bescoren' men – that is, shaved.

The argument began to arise between Christians in the East, who retained the tradition of beards, and those in the

West, who had adopted shaving. And the issue of beards was used as cover for a somewhat wider issue.

The great beard power struggle: Rome vs Constantinople

Christianity spread rapidly, thanks to the Romans. After a period of persecution under Nero, following the Great Fire of Rome in AD 64, and his successors, Emperor Constantine was the first to tolerate Christianity. He eventually converted after seeing a vision of a great cross in the sky with the words, 'In this sign, conquer,'[2] underneath, in around AD 312. While it is true that, from that point on, Christianity spread rapidly across the Roman Empire, what is considered far less is how the changes in the Roman Empire affected this spread.

By the time Constantine came to power, the Roman Empire was effectively two separate empires: West and East. Although Constantine became ruler of both, this conjunction was unstable and he was the last unified emperor.

Constantine had already moved his seat of power from Rome to Byzantium. He renamed it Constantinople, with the modesty one would expect of an emperor. It is now called Istanbul. Constantinople became the capital of the Empire for the next thousand years and quickly became engaged in a power struggle with Rome.

Rome claimed its Christian legacy from St Peter. In the canons (the laws of the Church that gradually grew up during the fourth and fifth centuries), Rome had established the papacy and the right to appoint bishops. Constantinople established a

---

[2] Constantine's version of Christianity was one in which God's favour would bring him success in battle, so not entirely in line with orthodox Christian beliefs.

patriarch who claimed the right to appoint bishops as well. Rome and the Western Empire was in rapid decline by the fourth and fifth centuries. By contrast, the Eastern Empire was growing in strength and would continue as the Byzantine Empire long after Rome was sacked by barbarians.[3]

And as these two sides of the Empire went their separate ways, so the two wings of the Church that operated under the respective auspices of Rome and Constantinople gradually went their separate ways. The ecumenical councils began to attract fewer bishops from 'the other side'. Practices in the Church began to vary.

Those in the East kept their beards. In many respects, they have consistently kept to the practice of Jesus and the teaching of the early church. Those in the Latin Church in the West, however, followed the example of Peter and the Romans and developed their own theology to base this on.

Beard laws

The first beard law allegedly came into the Church in AD 475 at the ecumenical council in Carthage. This stated that clerics must not allow either the hair on their heads or their beards to 'grow freely'. *Clericus nec comam nutriat nec barbam*[4] was the mantra. However, modern investigations have shown that this is highly likely to be an ancient form of fake news. The original text from the council was soon lost to the mists of time and the

---

[3] Rome was sacked at least six times. The first was by the Gauls in 390, then by Visigoths in 410, Vandals in 455 and Ostrogoths in 546. There was then a period of calm until the Normans sacked it again in 1084, and finally Charles V ransacked the city in 1527.

[4] This translates roughly as, 'Priests must not allow either their hair or their beards to grow freely.'

wonders of history. Copies from copies were all that remained. And those sneaky clerics who copied the text made a little change. They removed just one word from this sentence. *Radat* is the Latin word that means 'shave'. The scribes who made copies for distribution changed the meaning from saying that clerics must not shave to say that they must not let their beards grow. The exact opposite meaning. For this reason, we have no evidence that clerics of this time actually did shave, although the new meaning fitted much more conveniently with the convention of later times. It was useful for those in the Latin Church to claim this bit of history, so the myth persists.

Nevertheless, the Latin Church kept coming back to the issue. The Council of Aachen in 799, the Council of Bourges in 1031, the Council of Limoges in 1031 and the Council of Coyac in 1050 all mandated clerical shaving. The Council of Limoges even went as far as repeating the story about St Peter shaving and establishing the practice, proving that just because an ecumenical council says something, it does not make it true.

A whole range of other laws were passed concerning clerical behaviour at these councils, such as celibacy and eventually the ban on marriage and the rules concerning clerical dress. It is fascinating that, to Christians a thousand years ago, it was just as important, if not more so, for a priest to have a shaved head and face as it was for him to remain unmarried. Why one of those customs should have survived into the twenty-first century and the other should now be considered a peculiar quirk of history is far from obvious.

The Church in the Middle Ages

By the time we get to the mid-eleventh and twelfth centuries in Europe, Church and State had a close and mutually dependent relationship. Kings ruled by divine right – because God had declared that they should do so. In order to pull off this confidence trick on the population at large, they needed a compliant Church to go along with the wheeze. Popes, cardinals and bishops were therefore needed to confirm God's blessing on kings and those who claimed a right to kingship. When William of Normandy sought to stake his claim on the throne of England, for example, he first sought the approval of the pope so that he could claim that the crown was his by right in the eyes of God. When he landed on the beaches of Sussex in 1066, he did so under a papal banner.

In truth, it is hard to see a hard dividing line between Church and State in medieval Europe. It was hard for the medievals to see it too, so they had to work it out between them. After William's successful conquest of England, Pope Alexander II was delighted that he had backed the winner and no doubt felt he had made a significant contribution to the victory through his endorsement. Alexander wrote to William and invited him to Rome to pay homage. This was something William was pretty reluctant to do. In England, as in all of Europe, William had just acquired the right to appoint local bishops, as this had become a role adopted by the local nobility. Since William had just replaced the entire English nobility with his mates from Normandy, this effectively put the English Church in his pocket. The last thing he wanted to do was give up his new-found authority to the pope.

A few years later, in 1073, a new pope sought to wrestle back control of the Church from kings and nobles. Gregory VII set about professionalising the Church and putting kings in their place. One particularly troublesome king was Henry IV of Germany who had no interest in handing over his powers to a pope. So Gregory excommunicated Henry and released his subjects from the duty to obey him.

As a result, Henry arranged to meet Gregory to make peace and receive his welcome back. They were to meet high in the

Alps at Canossa Castle. Henry showed his penitence by walking barefoot from the village below to the castle to request an audience with the pope. For two days the pope refused, until he relented on the third and welcomed Henry back into the Church. Such was the relationship between Church and State.

In the years that followed, some tough constitutional work was done to figure out the boundaries between temporal and spiritual authority, and this became codified for the first time in 1107 under William the Conqueror's son, Henry I, in the Concordat of London. This said that the pope could appoint the bishops, but they would need to swear allegiance to the king, who ruled by divine right. A neat compromise all round.

But the eleventh and twelfth centuries were a funny old time for Christianity in Europe – because Europe was going through a funny old time. Spain was largely a Muslim country after North African Muslims invaded and defeated the Visigoths in the eighth century. Catholic Spain began its fightback in the eleventh century. In central Europe, just as the Muslims were defeating the Visigoths, Charlemagne was consolidating power and forming the Holy Roman Empire, which reached its height in the eleventh century. Just days before William the Conqueror defeated Harold in Hastings, Harold successfully quashed another invasion in the North from Vikings under Harald Hardrada, while Christianity was slowly taking hold in the Norse pagan lands of the Vikings. Harald Bluetooth declared Denmark to be Christian in AD 975, although in practice it took another 150 years or so for the country to become fully Christianised. For Christians in Europe, brief bouts of unity broke out around the Crusades, although these took a terrible toll in terms of money and lives.

In short, Europe was a turbulent, dangerous and confused place. And the same was true of the Church. While we think of it now as a single, centralised institution under the pope, this was only part of the picture. Theology and church practice were formally governed by the pope in the West and the patriarch in the East, but in reality local customs and practices varied. As a result, church teaching on beards was not always followed locally.

The beards that split the Church

The ante was really upped between the Eastern and Western Churches by a chap by the name of Photius. Or, as the Eastern Orthodox Church call him, Photius the Great. He had a huge impact on the Eastern Church, consolidating church law and reforming church structures.

Photius became Patriarch of Constantinople in AD 858, at a time when tensions between Rome and Constantinople were high and there were constant power struggles. His appointment was also rather complicated. The local bishops chose him to replace Ignatius following his exile after openly defying the Imperial family. But there was controversy when some refused to recognise Photius, preferring his predecessor in exile. So they appealed to the pope, who was happy to get involved, in an attempt to assert his authority in the East. Pope Nicholas I found a compromise where Photius stood down but would later be reconsidered when the appointment could be made in a more orderly fashion.

Photius chose to bide his time and agreed to the pope's plan, but the seeds were sown of a deep conflict between the pope and the patriarch. There were really two reasons for this conflict. The first was the issue of who was in charge. Photius and his supporters did not accept that the pope had primacy over the patriarch, while the pope wrote some fairly uncompromising letters stating that he did.

The other was a turf war. And that turf, specifically, was Bulgaria. Between the Christian lands of the Holy Roman

Empire in the West and the Byzantine Empire in the East lay the pagan countries of Central and Eastern Europe. Both the Eastern and Western Churches spotted the opportunity to expand their influence and the race was on to convert these people. Both the Latin Church and the Byzantine Church were sending missionaries there to convert the Bulgarians. As they sought to evangelise the locals, they became more concerned not with whether they would be loyal to Christ, but with whether they would be loyal to the pope or to the patriarch.

The fuel for this conflict between East and West was theology. The first and biggest issue was that the Latin Church had changed the Nicene Creed, a change that was formally adopted by the pope in 1014. The Creed was the foundation of the faith that had been agreed in the first Ecumenical Council in AD 325. It was a pretty big deal to change it, and the Eastern Church did not like it one bit.

The original Creed said that the Holy Spirit 'proceeded from the Father' but the Roman Church added a word: *filoque*. It's a relatively small word, but its theological implications were enormous, as this new, improved version of the Creed now said that the Holy Spirit 'proceeded from the Father *and the Son*'. This was the source of controversy for a few hundred years before the positions became so entrenched that it became the central issue around which the players in an East-vs-West power struggle could rally their troops.

Once the arguments got going, all sorts of supplementary and supportive disputes were thrown up. It seems that, just like today, once different groups set up sides against each other based on their identity, many and varied issues can be grasped to cause division between them. Some accusations were true and genuine points of difference; some were not. Western priests were not married and considered this an essential part of their calling to the priesthood, but Eastern priests were permitted to marry; true. Photius accused the Latins of eating eggs during Lent and thus breaking the Lenten fast; they did not. There were differences of practice related to fasting and feast days. And, of course, the Latins shaved. While other practices, such as the use of unleavened bread in Communion, priestly marriage and fasting get the profile now, the issue of shaving was raised again and again in these communications. In fact, Photius wrote to the pope to tell him that his habit of shaving was not very Christian.

THE BEARD QUESTION
SETTLING IT ONCE AND FOR ALL

TOSSING
A COIN

ROCK, PAPER,
SCISSORS

BEARDED V UNBEARDED
FOOTBALL MATCH

Roll forward to 1054, and the tensions between Rome and Constantinople reached a climax. A series of letters was exchanged between representatives of Pope Leo IX and the Patriarch, Michael I, arguing over a series of theological issues and, still, the primacy of the pope. The people were different and two hundred years had passed, but the basic situation was the same: they were arguing over who was in charge. And neither side was backing down. So Pope Leo decided to send one of his most senior cardinals to Constantinople to sort things out once and for all, endowed with the pope's full authority to act in his name.

It is considered unfortunate by historians that the man Leo chose to lead this mission was Cardinal Humbert. He was

rash, hot headed, ill-tempered and intransigent. Not exactly
the perfect diplomat. Or perhaps the ideal one if the outcome
you are looking for is a complete bust-up.

Things started badly when Humbert was unhappy with the
warmth of his welcome. Then he was accused of tampering
with the seals on the letters he brought from the pope (which
he had), and a dodgy Greek translation was provided for the
population at large to read. The version provided for general
consumption was an earlier draft, rather less civil in tone than
the final one.

Michael did not take this sort of behaviour well and refused
to discuss the substantive issues at all. Soon he refused to
speak with the pope's emissaries and resorted to blowing
raspberries at him from a balcony window.[5]

Humbert, not being a patient and understanding sort of
chap, responded to this by bursting into the Hagia Sophia, the
central church in Constantinople, and laying a Bull of
Excommunication on the altar in the name of the pope,
throwing Michael, Patriarch of Constantinople, out of the
Church and condemning him to hell.

It was an explosive document, setting out nine specific
charges of heresy against the patriarch. It kicked off with the
claim that the Eastern Church 'castrate their guests and
promote them not only to the clergy but to the episcopacy'.
There followed a series of allegations of theological error on
issues such as baptism and priestly marriage which amounted
to a series of heresies. It was alleged that the Eastern Church
rebaptised those already baptised like the Arian heretics. It
was alleged that Orthodox priests denied the effectiveness of
baptism conducted by Roman priests like Donatist heretics.

---

[5] OK, so I made that bit up, but it wasn't far off that in terms of
how childish the behaviour was and the determination to pick a
fight.

The proclamation concludes with the final devastating accusation that:

> They [Eastern Orthodox priests] grow the hair on their head and beards, they will not receive in communion those who tonsure their hair and shave their beards following the decreed practice of the Roman Church . . . Let them be anathema Maranatha with the Simoniacs, Valesians, Arians, Donatists, Nicolaitists, Severians, Pneumatomachoi, Manichaeans, Nazarenes, and all the heretics — nay, with the devil himself and his angels, unless they should repent. AMEN, AMEN, AMEN.

Humbert was clear that one of the main reasons to justify the excommunication of one of the most senior figures in Christianity worldwide was that he allowed his priests to grow beards. It was a sin that, among others, meant that, in the eyes of the pope, the patriarch was no better than the heretics and the devil himself. Of the nine allegations made, it is likely that only the fondness for facial hair and the permission for priests to marry were actually true. What is more, Pope Leo had actually died months before this Bull of Excommunication was written, so the authority for Humbert to issue it has been a source of fascination for historians ever since. The split in the Church between Orthodox and Catholics continues to this day, a thousand years later.

In return for this action, Michael excommunicated Humbert. The division in the Church was now irreconcilable. It would take another couple of hundred years before it was formally enshrined in church law, but this was the point of no return. So the year 1054 is known in the Church as 'The Great Schism'. While rival power struggles and increasing cultural and theological diversity were the sources, the issue of beard wearing was also one of the little-known factors that has largely been ignored by historians who struggle to understand why anyone would argue over it.

Top ten early church heresies

To give you an idea what those Orthodox Christians were up against, let's look at this week's runners and riders of early church heresies:

1. Arianism – the heresy that nearly took over the Church. Arians believed that Jesus was created by God and only called him his Son out of politeness. He was, they argued, a created being to whom God gave special powers.

2. Adoptionism – a heresy that has proved stubbornly tricky to kill off. This is the belief that Jesus was born a human and became divine at some point later on, after God put his Spirit into him.

3. Donatism – another big hitting heresy of its day. Donatists argued that Christian priests had to be sinless and faultless for the bread and wine they dished out to have any affect.

4. Marcionism – the belief that the God of the Old Testament and the God of the New Testament were actually two different Gods.

5. Apollinarism – the argument that Jesus had a human body but a divine mind.

6. *Gnosticism* – a whole group of heresies gang up to form Gnosticism, which taught that humans are made up of divine souls trapped in material bodies, so we should reject the material world in favour of the spiritual world.

7. *Pelagianism* – the belief that there is no original sin and humankind can choose to be sinless if we really want to without the aid of God.

8. *Nestorianism* – the belief that Jesus was just a man who had the Son of God somehow living in him.

9. *Monophysitism* – the belief that Jesus was wholly divine and not really human.

10. *Docetism* – a particularly creative heresy which argued that Jesus' body and his crucifixion were both an illusion. He was really a spiritual being who never died.

You would imagine that, with all this heresy kicking about in the Church, they would worry a bit less about facial hair and a bit more about basic Christian theology. But they seem to have adopted a form of theological 'zero tolerance' policy. If they allowed a bit of stubble today, it will be a roguish beard by the weekend and full-blown Gnosticism by next Thursday.

Relations between East and West remained tense right up until Western Christians sacked and pillaged Constantinople as they were passing through during the fourth Crusade in 1204. The sacking of Constantinople in 1204 by Western forces marked a turning point in the history of the Middle East. It fatally weakened the Byzantine Empire, leaving it unable to resist the inevitable invasion from the surrounding Arab Muslims. It would take another two hundred and fifty or so years before the unbreachable walls of the city were breached by Sultan Mehmet II in 1453.

But that is a different story. And it hardly made things less tense between the Catholic and Orthodox Churches, shall we say.

Middle-aged beards

Through the tenth and eleventh centuries, papal authorities kept coming back to the issue of how they could insist that their priests shaved. In 1080, Pope Gregory VII stamped his authority in the formerly Greek (i.e. Eastern) Church in Sardinia and wrote that he had forced the local archbishop to shave off his beard 'as the clergy of the whole Western Church have had the custom of shaving the beard from the very origins of the Christian faith'.[6] He forced all the clergy to follow suit.

In 1096, the Archbishop of Rouen stepped up the war against beards. He declared that any man with long hair or a beard would not only be excommunicated during his life, but also that he must not be prayed for after his death.

The Council of Toulouse, in 1119, threatened to excommunicate clerics who 'like a layman allowed hair and beard to grow', and Pope Alexander III said that any priests who allowed their beards to grow should be forcibly shaved by their archdeacon if they would not otherwise comply. The rule was inserted into canon law to make it extra official. William Durand, a thirteenth-century bishop and writer on canon law, explained the reason for all this follicle fighting:

---

[6] Jacques-Paul Migne, *Pope Gregory VII*, 1853.

The length of hair is symbolical of the multitude of sins. Hence clerics are directed to shave their beards; for the cutting of the hair of the beard, which is said to be nourished by the superfluous humours of the stomach, denotes that we ought to cut away the vices and sins which are a superfluous growth in us. Hence we shave our beards that we may seem purified by innocence and humility and that we may be like the angels who remain always in the bloom of youth.[7]

So, in a sense, the longer the beards, the more sinful you were thought to be. And attempts to enforce shaving among priests in the Western Church were therefore about reinforcing the purity of priests, as distinct from the laity who were sinful, and bearded. And they needed to be marked out from the Eastern Orthodox (bearded) heretics, too.

HEATHEN   INFIDEL

The beard that cost a cardinal the papacy

In 1455, the Catholic cardinals were in a conclave to elect a new pope. Nicholas V had died after eight years on the throne of St Peter. The early rounds of voting showed a split among the cardinals, based on Italian politics. Two factions were supporting different candidates for political reasons, and it was clear that neither had enough votes to win. A compromise candidate was

---

[7] *Decretals of Gregory IX*, III.

needed. One Basilios Bessarion was the obvious choice. He had grown up in the East and been educated in Constantinople. He was not aligned to either of the politicians. He was reliably neutral, was proposed and, in the next round, gathered support.

But there was a problem. He had a beard and refused to shave it off. Bessarion hoped to bring unity between the Eastern Orthodox Church and the Roman Church, and he kept some of the Eastern Orthodox customs from his youth as a symbol of this unity.

It was reported that a French cardinal made the fatal intervention:

> *Shall we select for Pope, for head of the Latin Church, a Greek, a mere interloper? Bessarion still wears his beard – and forsooth, he is to be our Lord! Hoe poor, then, must be our Latin Church if we can find no worthy man in it, but must needs resort to a Greek.*[8]

He just was not Roman enough, and the beard proved it. Bessarion responded that he didn't want to be pope anyway, and he was out of the running. Callixtus III was then elected as the Church's first Spanish pope. He was unquestionably Roman and completely bald.

Despite the comments made in the conclave, Bessarion remained a well-respected senior cardinal and was considered again as a candidate after Callixtus died in 1464. But he never shaved his beard, and never became pope.[9]

---

[8] Artaud de Montor, *The Lives and Times of the Popes*, (1911), pp. 147–9.

[9] As a footnote in history it is worth noting that Bessarion left his mark in another important way. After his upbringing in the East, he took with him to the Vatican a keen interest in astronomy. During his time there, he gathered around him others who developed the field of astronomy, subsequently inspiring the work of Copernicus and Galileo.

THE EXCEPTION THAT PROVES THE RULE

While the early Catholic Church was very much a shaved institution, there was one group that bucked this trend.

In 1525, Matteo da Bascio, a Fransiscan friar, found himself moved to imitate the life of St Francis of Assisi more closely. He looked at the way of life in his monastery and decided that it was not sufficiently solitary or penitent. His superiors did not like the idea of change, however, and his arguments fell on deaf ears. In spite of this, Friar Matteo and a number of his companions sought new ways of living within the monastery. This was initially disastrous as he was accused of abandoning his religious duties and his superiors made to arrest them. They were forced into hiding and found refuge with another order of monks, the Camaldolese.

By 1528, Friar Matteo had appealed to the top, and Pope Clement VII gave him permission to live as a hermit. He took to wearing a brown cloak with a hood in tribute to the Camaldolese monks who had given him shelter. The new order took its name from the hood on the cloak – the Capuchin.

Capuchin monks tried to live like St Francis as literally as possible. One of these ways was to grow a beard. In 1529 they formalised their rules, which included the stipulation that Capuchin monks must never shave.

6

Hairy Non-Christians

It is not only Christians who have a religious basis for their beards, of course. Muslims, Sikhs and Hindus all have religious duties concerning their beards. We have seen that beards have had religious significance since the dawn of civilisation, so it should be no surprise that all the world's major religions have something to say on the topic.

As we have seen with different Christian groups, the beard has been a way of developing cultural unity among adherents and of expressing God's relationship with mankind. They have all approached the topic from their own perspectives, but the extent to which facial hair appears universally to have spiritual significance is remarkable.

The holy Roman moustache

Historically speaking, beards have come and gone in and out of fashion over the centuries. The moustache, however, has been a much rarer creature.

Occasional moustaches have been spotted on statues or paintings in early history. For example, a statue of the Fourth Dynasty Egyptian Prince Rahotep (c. 2550 BC) shows him with a distinctly hairy upper lip.

The first widespread moustaches in recorded history were described in the diary of Julius Caesar. After Caesar had conquered Gaul, he spotted another land over the sea when he stood at the northerly coast. It was England. In 54 BC he took a small force over to investigate this new land and recorded what he found in his diary.

When he landed in Kent, he was surprised by the people he met. No doubt they had an inkling that this visitor was potentially dangerous, so they put on a show. He wrote in his diary, 'All the Britons, indeed, dye themselves with wood, which occasions a bluish colour, and thereby have a more terrible appearance in fight. They wear their hair long and have every part of their body shaved except their head and upper lip.' It is highly unlikely that they dyed themselves blue every day, but, since you cannot grow a moustache overnight, this was likely their normal custom.

Honourable mention for the noblest moustache in history must be given to the Holy Roman Emperor, Father of Europe, King of the Franks, Charlemagne: Charles the Great.

Charlemagne was the eldest son of Pepin the Short. But do not let that title fool you. Pepin had big ambitions. When he died in AD 768, Charles co-ruled the Frankish Kingdom (parts of modern Germany, France and Belgium) with his brother Carloman I, who died in mysterious circumstances a few years later. With Charles now sole ruler, he set to work expanding his territories east and west. He Christianised the Saxons to the west on pain of death and led excursions into Muslim Spain. In AD 800, Charlemagne was crowned Emperor of the Romans by Pope Leo III on Christmas Day in Old St Peter's Basilica.

Charles was a big supporter of the Latin pope. So you might have thought he would go for the clean-shaven look favoured at the time by the Church of Rome. But Charles was a canny operator, and realised that he needed to keep his power base at home happy too. His alliance with the pope gave him a purpose around which he could rally the troops and gave him legitimacy as a man acting on God's wishes. But he needed to show he was still a man of his people, the Franks.

The Franks were a hairy people. Hairiness was a sign of social status, with the higher strata of society being permitted to wear their hair and beards long. Frankish rulers were often known as the 'long-haired kings'. Charlemagne did not want to lose this identity, but he did want to merge it with the Catholic faith and the Roman Empire. So he went halfway. He shaved his beard, wore his hair to his shoulders and kept a moustache. Just enough Frank to show he was one of the boys, but shaved enough to show he was a devout Christian in the Latin Church and heir to the Roman emperors of the past.

Charlemagne's eldest son is also worthy of note here too. Pepin the Hunchback was disinherited by charlemagne when his mother lost favour and Charlemagne divorced her. When Pepin grew older, he launched a rebellion against his father, which was quickly put down with little damage done. Charlemagne had mercy on his son and commuted his death sentence. Instead, he shaved him. Pepin was given the clerical tonsure – his face and the top of his head were shaved – and sent to a monastery. The Frankish warlords would never follow a tonsured man, so he was no longer a threat.

The beards of other faiths

While the focus of this story is the fascinating and complex relationship Christians have had with their facial follicles, it would be foolish in the extreme to pass over entirely the views of the other great faiths. Many faiths have long and distinguished histories of being bearded, so we should examine the origins of these beliefs, as well as note the influence they have had.

Islam

Muslim men are bearded. However, debate rages within the faith as to whether this is a recommendation or a requirement. The sources on this topic are disputed, although the consensus for Sunni Muslims is that the beard is compulsory.

There is no doubt that the Prophet Mohammed had a beard. Some Muslim scholars have argued that this is, in itself, sufficient cause for others to follow suit and do likewise. However, there is a far more interesting story to be told.

Islam has a number of holy texts, which carry greater or lesser authority. The Qur'an is the ultimate authority, believed to be the words of Allah himself as dictated to the Prophet Mohammed. Alongside the Qur'an sits the Tawrat (Torah), the Zabur (Psalms) and the Injil (Gospel), as well as the Scrolls of Abraham and Moses. The Qur'an also contains interpretations and commentary given by early Muslim Scholars. The Muslim faith is complex.

Surprisingly, however, there are in all these texts few clear prescriptions concerning the beard. Given how important it is considered to be for many adherents, there are few explicit mentions of shaving or cultivating the beard in Muslim scholarship.

One sura (chapter, or section) of the Qur'an states, 'And most certainly I [Shaytan] will lead them astray and excite in them vain desires, and bid them that they shall slit the ears of the cattle, and most surely I will bid them so that they shall alter Allah's creation, and whoever takes the Satan for a guardian rather than Allah he indeed shall suffer a manifest loss' (The Women/al-Nisa, chapter 4, verse 119). The reference here to 'alter Allah's creation' is often taken to mean altering the body, which, therefore, would include the beard. But the reference is oblique at best.

The clearest story comes from one of the narrations on the sayings of the Prophet Mohammed. Allamah Majlisi quotes in a narration, in volume 16 of his book *Bihar al-Anwar* (*Seas of Illuminations*), the Prophet Muhammad saying:

> *When Allah, the Blessed, the Merciful, accepted the repentance of Adam, Gabriel came to Adam and said, 'May Allah grant you a (long) life and bestow beauty upon you.' Adam then said, 'I understand what you mean by long life, however, I do not understand what you mean by beauty.' [Thus, in thanking Allah, his Lord and Master] he went into prostration and when he raised his head from it, he made a supplication and said, 'O, Allah, increase in me the beauty [that you have promised me].' Soon after he had made the supplication a beautiful beard appeared on his radiant face. When Gabriel witnessed what had happened, he touched the beard of prophet Adam and said, 'This is in response to the supplication you made to your Lord, and it has been granted to you and your male offspring till the day of reckoning.'*

In this version of the creation story, Adam asked God to make him beautiful and the response was a beard. Ergo, God thinks beards are beautiful.

There are a number of stories in Islamic oral tradition which appear to show that, from the earliest days of Islam, it has been considered the rule that men would wear a beard. And the reason is simple: God made you that way and you should not mess around with God's creation.

Islam is the world's second most followed religion, with 1.8 billion adherents, after Christianity's 2.4 billion. That makes the Muslim nations of the world by far the greatest contributors to our planet's stock of facial hair.

Hinduism

Christianity and Islam have a clear point in history when the faiths were founded. By contrast, Hinduism emerged from a number of traditional religions in the Indian subcontinent in the millennia before Jesus' birth. Classical Hinduism as we know it today emerged around 500 BC, and is the world's third most popular faith, with 1.2 billion adherents.

Thiruthani Temple is a Hindu temple, on the hill of Thiruttani, Tamil Nadu, in India. It is dedicated to the commander of the gods, Kartikeya, the god of victory and war. The temple performs all the normal functions of a Hindu temple, but with one particular added speciality: every year it collects tons and tons of human hair. Pilgrims from across India visit Thiruthani to offer their hair to the gods for good luck. This is done in imitation of the god Vishnu, according to one Hindu myth.

Vishnu was hit on the head with an axe. An angel called Neela Devi offered him a lock of her hair to cover the wound. This had the effect of healing it instantly and covering the missing hair on his head. Vishnu was delighted and declared that anyone who offered their hair to the gods as a sacrifice would be granted their wishes. To this day, Hindus offer their hair to the gods when in urgent need, and the temple at Thiruthani is one of the places they go to do it.

Most Hindu men do not shave, and many do not cut their hair at all, although the traditions followed depend on which of the deva (gods) and other teachings are followed. In general, the sadhus, yogis and other holy men wear beards, although Vaishnava men usually shave as a sign of cleanliness.

Sikhism

Another faith that mandates the beard is Sikhism. Sikhs are in no doubt on this matter.

Sikhism was founded in around AD 1500 by Guru Nanak Dev. It is a monotheistic religion which believes that everything is part of god and that god is part of everything. Sikhs therefore focus on an alignment between the physical and the metaphysical, to break the cycle of birth and rebirth and become one with god.

The tenth Sikh Guru, Gobind Singh, spelt out clearly that Sikhs cannot cut their hair. Any of it. Ever. Kesh, uncut hair, is one of the five compulsory articles of faith for a baptised Sikh. The core of this belief is similar to that of the early Christians and Muslims: hair is part of God's good creation. But more than that, the pursuit of oneness with God and the belief that God is in everything means that to cut, damage or destroy any of that good creation is to cut, damage or destroy a part of God himself.

The traditional beliefs of India – Sikhism, Hinduism and other local beliefs – had a major influence on British facial hair when the British set up shop in India as the colonial power. But you will have to wait a little for that chapter in the story.

7

Beards in Heaven and Hell

Will people have beards in heaven or will we have to shave there? Christians have spent a lot of time considering what it will take to be welcomed into heaven, when the time comes. And many have speculated on the nature of the heavenly realm and on the nature of the bodies the faithful will have when they are resurrected. So the question of whether men will be bearded in heaven must be addressed. Those who consider shaving a painful and time-consuming activity may have mixed feelings on the matter. Luckily, one medieval theologian has the answer for us.

Conversely, you may wonder about the facial fate of those condemned to eternity in a fiery furnace. Since Christians have spent two thousand years debating whether men should wear beards or not, it is rather curious that they should have come to consistently depict the devil with a goatee. And that is where we will begin.

Beards in hell: the devil's goatee

There is one beard that requires special attention in the history of Christian thought: that of the devil. The most common depiction of Satan today is that of a red figure with horns and hooves, carrying a pitchfork and sporting a dandyesque goatee and moustache. This image took centuries to come about. How and why it did reveals a lot about the preoccupations of those who represented the devil this way.

One of the earliest images of a recognisable devil is contained in the *Codex Gigas*, the Giant Book. It is the largest surviving medieval manuscript of the Bible and dates from the thirteenth century. It is also known as the devil's Bible as it contains an illustration of the devil, which was highly unusual. The image would be recognisably Satanic to any modern reader – a red man with horns. He has claws on his hands and feet, but in this image he has a green face and is not carrying a pitchfork.

It was during the Middle Ages when images of the devil suddenly began to emerge. The Church at the time was struggling to explain to people why their worship was failing to protect them from the devastation of plague that had swept from Asia right across Europe. The effect was profound. Many clergy simply fled plague-affected areas. Those who stayed and cared for the sick contracted the disease themselves and died. Priests and doctors had no explanation for this terrible curse. By the mid-fourteenth century, around half the entire population of Europe succumbed to the Black Death.

Some argued that the plague was God's wrath on the people in response to their sins. The flagellant movement emerged, whereby people would publicly whip themselves as an act of penitence to try to ward off the plague. Church bells would be rung to try to hold back the mysterious disease.

It is often said, however, that one should never let a good crisis go to waste. And the Church realised that the sudden and mysterious death of large numbers of people could be an opportunity for evangelism. They began to ask whether people knew where they would go if they should die. Are they sure they would go to heaven? And how much time would they have to spend in purgatory to atone for their sins? They also saw a financial opportunity, to charge the terrified populace for their services and to ensure that worldly wealth was left to the Church after death. This would guarantee God's favour when he had to make his mind up about admission through the Pearly Gates. To make the choice more stark, stories of torture at the hands of the devil abounded, to demonstrate the fate that awaited those unwilling to pay up.

Fear of death in such dangerous times is most understandable, and fascination with what would come next led artists and writers to use their imaginations. Images of the devil suddenly appeared everywhere, as varied as they were numerous. In medieval art the devil is often depicted as blue or green, with or without horns and in all manner of forms. Since there are no indications in the Bible as to the devil's appearance, artists had to use their imaginations. The only biblical image for the devil is the story of the snake tempting Adam and Eve in the Garden of Eden. And so the devil was often portrayed with snakes wrapped around him and even emerging from his body.

A SUSPICIOUS GOATEE

Over time, artists also began to use images of popular culture to portray the devil. Images from pagan gods were used, just as they had been used earlier to represent Jesus. The trident is most commonly associated with the Greek god Poseidon, who used it as a deadly weapon and as an instrument of his power to perform miraculous acts on earth. Thus, it was the perfect tool for the devil to use to torture souls in the underworld.

As early as AD 300, another pagan god began to be associated with the devil. Pan was the god of nature, a shepherd who was half-man and half-goat. He was the god of fertility and was associated with spring. He was a largely benevolent figure in Greek and Roman mythology, and because he was half-goat, naturally he had horns and a goatee beard.

As Christians sought to convert the pagans, however, they found ways to show the evil in these otherwise benign figures. Pan was closely associated with one particular topic which Christians would be famous for struggling with up to the present day: sex. Pan was known for his sexual prowess and was often depicted with a large phallus.

Prudish Christians sought to demonise Pan as a result. The association grew during the Renaissance as interest in classical mythology re-emerged and, in due course, the image of half-man half-goat who sought his own pleasure no matter the cost would become part of the standard image of the devil. It was not until the Victorian era, when interest in classical art and literature reached its height, that the image of the devil as a Pan-like figure became consistently adopted. And, with it, the goatee beard would forever become demonic.

Beards in heaven

An interesting point arises in Christian theology when considering the topic of beards. Will men have beards in heaven?

Since the very earliest times, orthodox Christian belief has been that there will be a resurrection of believers. In other words, after their death, believers will rise again and live in the world to come. This resurrection will follow Jesus' own resurrection and will be a physical, bodily one. Christ was able to show the wounds in his hands and side to Doubting Thomas as evidence that it really was him, proving that the resurrection was not only physical but would bear some relation to our own current bodies.

The details of this have been much debated, and one question has yet to be resolved: will we have our beards? We alight on this particular theological platform at this precise moment because it became a matter of debate in 1160 in the middle of a heated beard controversy in France.

The Cistercians were one of the largest groups of monks in the Middle Ages. Their monasteries had a mantra of 'work hard, pray hard',[1] and they were widely respected across Europe. There were two ranks of brothers in Cistercian monasteries: the monks and the lay brothers. Lay brothers were basically junior monks. Usually less educated, they were not ordained clerics like the monks. As a result, the lay brothers were often looked down upon and they were given the menial jobs in the monastery to do and not the holy offices. While some would think the Cistercians might see the most menial tasks as the highest calling, nevertheless, tensions between lay brothers and monks could arise.

It was easy to tell the difference between a monk and a lay brother, both because the monks had robes of a slightly lighter shade and because the monks shaved, while the lay brothers did not. In 1160, a run-in between Abbot Burchard of Bellevaux and the lay brothers in his monastery led to the world's first book on beards: *Apologia de Barbis*, an explanation of beards.

Accusations of impropriety and bad behaviour by the lay brothers of Bellevaux's sister monastery, Rosière, had reached

---

[1] Needless to say, but for the avoidance of any doubt, this is not actually their motto, but The Church Mouse's précis of their general attitude and philosophy. Apologies for any confusion.

the ears of Abbot Burchard. So he wrote to them to put them straight. Burchard referenced the prophet Isaiah's comment that a garment mixed with blood would become fuel for the fire. Since the lay brothers were accused of fighting, he warned them that their beards may become fuel for the fire.

If this was an attempt at medieval banter, it did not go down well. The lay brothers heard this as a threat to burn off their beards if they misbehaved again. As a result, the tension rose, and Abbot Burchard decided to write a treatise on the topic of the beard as a final word on the matter.

Apologia de Barbis is masterful. It is absurd in its claims and wildly ambitious in its prose. Burchard attempts to praise the beards of the lay brothers and extols their virtues at length. He draws on the natural philosophy of the early church fathers, setting out that the beard was a symbol of the virtue of man:

> *A beard is appropriate to a man as a sign of his comeliness, as a sign of his strength, as a sign of his wisdom, as a sign of his maturity and as a sign of his piety. And when these things are equally present in a man, he can justly be called full-bearded, since his beard shows him to be not a half-man or womanly man, but a complete man, with a beard that is plentiful on his chin and along his jaw and under his chin.*

At this point, however, Burchard backs himself into a philosophical corner. If beards are so great, how come the monks shaved them off? The answer was that they grew inner beards. It was what was inside that mattered more than outward appearances. Just as it was more important to have faith than merely to go through the motions, so it was more important to have the virtues the beard represented than to have the beard itself. Bishop Bruno had made the same argument a few years earlier:

Men who are strong are superior to those who only wish to seem so. Therefore, let our interior beard grow, just as the exterior is shaved; for the former grows without impediment, while the latter, unless it is shaved, creates many inconveniences and is only nurtured and made beautiful by men who are truly idle and vain.[2]

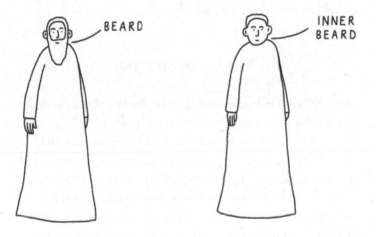

Burchard argued that, while the beard was a symbol of virtue, it was also a source of temptation to vanity. So a monk in pursuit of the highest calling might shave off the beard and embrace the outwardly embarrassing appearance in order to avoid the temptation to vanity, and thereby cultivate the inner beard of goodness. He advised the lay brothers to let their beards grow unkempt and be 'neglected in rustic lack of fashion'.

In the culmination of his great work, Burchard considered beards in the afterlife. He concluded that men will stop shaving in the world to come and all will be bearded. When we rise

[2] Quoted by Giles Constable in his introduction to R. B .C. Huygens (ed.), *Gozechini Epistola ad Walcherum. Burchardi . . . Apologia de barbis : Apologiae duae* (Turnholti: Typographi Brepols, 1985).

to be with the Lord, the temptation to vanity will fall away and the inner beard of virtue will be complete. We will have both inner and outer beards in heaven.

It is hard to tell if this calmed the lay brothers down. But it has left the world with a masterpiece of medieval theology on the topic of beards. And the answer to our opening question: men will be bearded in heaven.[3]

THE SIN OF SHAVING

The division between clerics, who had to shave, and the laity, who were not permitted to, is perfectly illustrated by a story recorded by Otloh of St Emmeram in 1032. The story goes that a distinguished man was accused of the crime of stealing a horse. Attempting to prove his innocence, he submitted himself to 'trial by water', whereby floating was deemed to be a failure of the test. The man indeed failed and was hence publicly 'proven' to be guilty, so he confessed his sin to the local priests and sought their advice on how to get himself off the hook.

Most of the priests pronounced their absolution after he confessed every sin he could think of, but one priest stood out, telling him, 'I myself see a great sin upon you which you neither revealed to us in confessing nor believe to be a sin. For although you are a layman and should go about with your beard unshaven in the manner of laymen, you have nevertheless, in contempt of divine law, shaved your beard just like a cleric. Truly such a sin, although you regard it as nothing, I believe

---

[3] Well, according to Abbot Burchard at least. This Mouse is not convinced.

to be so great that you shall in no way be absolved from the crime into which you have fallen unless you do penance and promise God to avoid such behaviour from now on.'

Now, having confessed and had forgiveness pronounced, the man's trial was repeated and his innocence this time demonstrated; he got away with merely having to pay for the horse he had pinched. And they all lived happily ever after, particularly the young man, who immediately went back to shaving once he was out of the hot seat.

Banning beards

In 1979, the Scottish football champions Celtic drew Partizani Tirana, Albania, in the first round of the European Cup. This is what soccer pundits refer to as a 'tricky away tie'. Right back Danny McGrain, the team talisman, had taken over as captain the previous year after Kenny Dalglish had left for Liverpool. He would make more than 650 competitive appearances for Celtic in his career and amass a cupboardful of trophies. The build-up to the game was dominated by one question: would McGrain be allowed into Albania. The problem was that McGrain was famously bearded and Albania had a strict ban on beards. Would he play with a beard? Would he shave it for the game? In the end, the Albanians allowed McGrain and his beard into the country, but did him the discourtesy of beating them both 1–0.[4]

---

[4] It was a truly bizarre game. For fear of the quality of the local food, the Celtic players took their own food on the trip. Danny McGrain took a loaf of bread, a pack of gammon and a dozen tea bags. The

In 1967, the People's Republic of Albania formally became an atheist state, picking up the mantle from other Communist regimes in their attempt to eliminate religion. A new constitution was introduced and the ruling regime in Albania, under the dictator Enver Hoxha, embraced the project with a zeal that one could only describe as . . . religious. The new laws were wide-ranging and penalties for transgressions harsh, up to and including death. All religious buildings were nationalised and converted for other uses. More than two hundred clerics were imprisoned, with some being starved to death or executed. In 1972, the Catholic priest Shtjefën Kurti was executed for secretly baptising a child.

Beards were also prohibited. The predominant religion in Albania was Islam, with around two-thirds of the country adhering to some form of it. Since this required the wearing of a beard, banning facial hair was part and parcel of outlawing religion. Albania was also setting its face against the West, where the hippy movement had emerged in the 1960s. So banning beards was also part of the general ban on all things Western, including the miniskirt, rock and roll and surrealist art. While a ban on beards was another nail in the coffin of individual freedom, it did provide a boon to razor blade manufacturers. Having said that, the communist regime brought near total economic collapse to the country, so they did not make much of a profit from this increased level of demand, albeit legally mandated.

---

performance foods of their day. The Albanian national anthem was played through the stadium tannoy at regular intervals during the game and the Scottish press were not given visas to travel, so members of the Scottish squad had to file reports with the media back home. The Tirana players' shirts were all a slightly different shade of red and had numbers painted on the back in white paint. The crowd in the stadium was mute for much of the game, fuelling fears that they had been forced to attend by the government.

When it comes to banning beards, however, Albania is possibly the only state that has attempted to enforce a total ban at the national level under criminal law. In Tajikistan, police were accused of forcing Muslims to shave their beards as part of a clampdown from the secularist government on Islam in the country in 2015. While the state does ban what it considers to be foreign-sounding names, birthday parties outside the home and loud crying at funerals, the ban on beards is officially non-existent. But in both Albania and Tajikistan, the anti-beard mood was explicitly religious in origin.

There is some speculation that North Korea currently has a beard ban. It has been widely reported that all North Koreans must select from a short list of state-approved haircuts. While there are no mentions of beards in these reports, this author cannot trace a picture of a single North Korean with any facial hair whatsoever, so is prepared to draw the conclusion that the Dear Leader does not approve. The official legal status, however, is not known.

The shaving ban

Ivan Vasilyevich was not someone you would want to cross. He became tsar of all Russia in 1547 and established a reputation that gave him the nickname which is best translated into modern English as Ivan the Formidable. It is perhaps more appropriate to call him by his more familiar name: Ivan the Terrible.

Ivan was a complex character, simultaneously pious, devout and a psychotic mass murderer. His reign was marked by a totalitarian control over the lives of his people. The Orthodox faith was a key reason for his control and also a means by which he exerted it; Ivan believed that God had put him on the

throne of Russia. That gave him a sacred duty to punish oppo-
nents, and he dreamed up ways to do this that echoed the
expected torments of hell. He was a prolific torturer, known
to boil his victims alive, freeze them to death, drown them or
otherwise brutalise them. In a fit of rage, he even murdered his
own son and heir.

Given the importance that we have seen the Orthodox
faith ascribed to the beard, this was one cause that Ivan
embraced with gusto. He famously said, 'To shave the beard
is a sin that the blood of all the martyrs cannot cleanse.' All
male Russian citizens therefore had to wear a beard. Failing
to do so was not only an offence against Ivan, but also an
offence against God.

This was broadly accepted by Ivan's subjects. The Orthodox
faith had adapted well into Russia and the people were fond
of their religion. Shortly after Ivan's death, the position of
Bishop of Moscow was elevated to that of Patriarch of
Moscow and all Rus'. The first to occupy that position,
Patriarch Job, also briefly became head of state.

Russia's mix of Church and State remains closely inter-
twined right up to the present day. Tsarist regimes laid claim
to the Church to justify their grip on power. While the post-
revolutionary communist powers attempted to stamp out the
Church, they ultimately failed, and the present regime has
allied itself once more with the Russian Orthodox Church.

In the sixteenth century, the assertion of religiously inspired
imperial power meant mandatory beards for the people. In
due course, the tables would turn, however.

The beard tax

History records just one instance of a beard tax. We will remain
in Russia but skip forward two hundred years to Peter I's Russia.

The year is 1698, to be precise. Russia is a global military power and her tsars are international statesmen. But there is a problem: Russia is still a feudal society in an age when industry is revolting – by which I mean the industrial revolution is just getting moving. Across Europe, countries are urbanising, innovating, expanding through colonialisation and generally upping their game. In Russia, however, the economic system relies on the same arrangements of peasant farmers tied in serfdom to a local land-owning aristocrat that has been in place for centuries.

This lack of development was something that the young Peter I wanted to address as soon as he took the throne. It was just embarrassing for Peter, who needed to keep up with the Joneses.[5]

And address it he did. Peter would later be known as Peter the Great for the impact he had in setting Russia's course towards modernisation. He would go on to reform Russia's calendar, script, culture, economy and society. By the mid-eighteenth century, Russia was a world leader in opera, ballet, music and art, and a major global economic and military power. All thanks to Peter.

In 1697, Peter set off on the Grand Embassy. This was a combined mission of diplomatic visits and fact finding. Peter visited almost all major European powers and all manner of economic, scientific, cultural and military innovators, manufacturers and establishments. While he was visiting England, he took in the Royal Observatory, the Royal Mint, the Royal

---

[5] William III on the throne in England, Ireland, Scotland and parts of Holland; Louis XIV was strutting his stuff in France and becoming the 'Sun King'; and Leopold I was conquering his way to being not only Holy Roman Emperor but also King of Hungary, Croatia and Bohemia. The Joneses were quite hard to keep up with.

Society and the University of Oxford, along with several ship-yards and military manufacturing plants. He observed a session in the Houses of Parliament. To help his studies, he travelled undercover as Sergeant Pyotr Mikhaylov and even spent time working in the Royal Navy dockyard in Deptford and the Dutch East India Company dockyards to learn first-hand about ship building.

The tour was largely a diplomatic failure, but a huge success in terms of how much Peter learned about the latest trends in Europe. He loved it and returned with 260 chests full of items he had collected on his travels. His conclusion was that Russia needed to modernise and become more European, throwing off the shackles of Russia's feudal past and embracing a new industrial future along European lines.

On his return to Russia in 1698, Peter was met by the Commander in Chief of his army, government ministers and numerous high-ranking members of society. He received their welcome, but then produced a razor and – to their alarm – started shaving the men who had lined up to greet him.

Along with the economic structure and industry, Peter saw the hair on his people's faces as something in need of reform. The Russian preference for a long beard had to change. While he made an exception in the case of Orthodox priests, Peter wanted everyone else to look just like modern, hip and trendy Europeans, which meant they should shave. Peter duly declared that all Russians should lose their beards.

Heavily influenced by the Orthodox Church, Russians had come to see the beard as a sign of masculinity and viril-ity. In laying the foundations for his assault on the beard, however, Peter had taken the precaution of abolishing the patriarchate of Moscow and all Rus', and had taken direct control of the Church, thereby reforming the Church as well as society.

Nevertheless, Peter's new shaving policy was massively unpopular, so he modified it. His new approach was to introduce a tax on beards instead of a total ban. Perhaps he thought that everyone loved a good tax. Or that there was no chance that the put-upon proletarian masses would ever rise up in rebellion against the injustices wrought upon them by their feudal masters.[6]

The system was introduced whereby anyone with a beard could be stopped in the street and summarily shaved unless they were able to produce their beard tax token. This copper coin bore the slogan, 'The beard is a superfluous burden,' just to make sure those who chose to pay the tax got the message.

While it had the benefit of raising much-needed funds for the imperial coffers, taxing an already impoverished peasant class is not the sort of thing that sees your opinion poll ratings increase. In fact, the beard tax had some perverse results. The rich saw it as something of a status symbol. They could demonstrate on their faces that they were happy to pay the tax, and so the beard became an increasingly fashionable item for the wealthy classes. Those who were poorer were forced to shave and resented the imposition. One has to feel a certain sympathy for their plight. By 1707, the tax was abolished, having achieved little.

It can prove difficult to change opinions on deep-seated cultural beliefs. Even today, these attitudes to beards persist in Russia. In 2017, Metropolitan Kornily, Primate of the Russian Orthodox Old Believer Church, declared that it was terrible to see fashions moving away from the traditional Russian beard and that men should keep their beards to 'protect them from homosexuality'.

---

[6] To be fair, it would be almost 150 years before they did, by which time Peter the Great was long dead and not at all bothered.

FAKE NEWS ALERT : FAKE NEWS ALERT : FAKE NEWS

This is a public service announcement on the topic of beard taxes. Your humble author would like to draw your attention to an unfounded internet rumour. If you should encounter this rumour at any point henceforth you have permission to look down on the perpetrator of this falsehood with a sense of intellectual superiority and to shout 'fake news' as loudly as you like.

It is often claimed that Henry VII introduced a beard tax and that this tax was later revived by his daughter Elizabeth I. The origin of this fable is unknown. What *is* known is that it has been rejected by historians who have found no contemporaneous evidence that it existed. Henry was bearded, and portraits of the day show many to be similarly hairy-faced. While Elizabeth I did introduce strict guidelines on clothing and dress in court, this did not include any strictures on beards, moustaches, sideburns, goatees or any other form of facial hair.

FAKE NEWS ALERT : FAKE NEWS ALERT : FAKE NEWS

PART IV

THE BIG RELIGIOUS BEARD COMEBACK

8

History's Holiest Beards

By the sixteenth century, the beard was well and truly back in Europe. There had been plenty of twists and turns of history by then, so we will walk the long and winding path a little further through beard history and discover why medieval man loved a big soup strainer. We will see some of the greatest religious beards in history, from the Spanish warrior king El Cid to Henry VIII, and the great Protestant reformers, and finally the illicit beards of the popes, who really should have obeyed church law and shaved.

Crusaders' beards

The Crusades were terrible. Perhaps this does not need to be said. Or rather, this does not need to be said here in a discussion on the godliness or otherwise of facial hair. But it is hard to escape the importance of beards in the Crusades, or indeed the importance of the Crusades on the history of beards.

The Crusades took place over a two-hundred-year period between 1096 and 1291. Pope Urban II called upon the Christians of Europe to undertake the first Crusade in 1095. The mission was simple: to ensure pilgrims' access to the Holy Land, then under Muslim control, by reinforcing the Christian forces under the Byzantine Emperor in Constantinople.

But things are never that simple. What was really going on was a pretty toxic mix of realpolitik, the pursuit of wealth and power, and religious zeal. Some Crusaders were fired up by the call to protect Christendom from the heathen armies of the East and the promise of God's favour for those who joined; others were somewhat more pragmatic and saw war as a means for personal gain. Popes and kings were vying for position and used the rabble-rousing power of Crusader spirit to further their own causes. Perhaps most interestingly, the popes may also have had an eye on reuniting the Western and Eastern Churches, following the split in 1054. By reunification, they did not mean in a noble sense, of course, but rather the subjugation of East by West through the projection of military power.

The battle for supremacy between the Eastern and Western Church came to a tragic head during the fourth Crusade, when Western Crusaders sacked Constantinople in an act of unspeakable savagery. For three days the Crusaders ran amok in the city, looting, vandalising, murdering and raping. Holy sites were not spared. Nor were the clerics inside them. The great library of Constantinople was destroyed.

One treasure that still survives from that looting is a set of bronze horses from the Hippodrome. Today they sit on the façade of the Basilica San Marco in St Mark's Square, Venice, after Venetian Crusaders took them home.

In the early days of the Crusades, it was easy to tell the Crusaders from the Muslim armies they were fighting, as the Crusaders were all clean shaven, while the Muslims sported the traditional long beard. In 1190, one of Sultan Saladin's supply ships managed to sneak through the Crusaders' blockade by pretending to be crewed by Westerners. They let pigs roam the deck and shaved their beards. The deception worked a treat.

But during the course of the Crusades, things began to change for the Westerners. They started to grow beards. Perhaps because life was hard while at war, or perhaps because they became more used to the local customs of the Eastern Orthodox Christians, they began to adopt the beard.

One of the most famous groups of Crusaders was the Knights Templar, a religious order founded in 1119. Templars were essentially monks whose calling from God, so they believed, was to be kick-ass warriors. After the successful first Crusade, the Templars formed a permanent military presence for the Church to protect the surrounding areas of Jerusalem. They became hugely wealthy and among the finest fighters in the Crusades. In 1170, five hundred Templars defeated a Muslim army of twenty-six thousand.

The Templars were distinguished for wearing beards. It is not known why they did this or when it started, but it appears to have been quite early in the development of their order. The most likely reason is that the beards gave them a more fearsome appearance in battle.

The Rule of the Templar governed the conduct of the Knights, and it gave specific instruction to wear the tonsure (shaving the top of the head to leave a 'crown' of hair) and to keep their beards neat and tidy. They also had a prohibition on pointy shoes.[1]

Of course, once the toughest and wealthiest of the Crusaders became bearded, others were sure to follow. It was still the practice in the West to shave, however. This led to a rather tragic turn of events in 1290. A group of Italian Crusaders arrived in the Holy Land, eager for a fight. Assuming that anyone with a beard was a Muslim, they went on a killing

---

[1] The fashion of the time included very elongated pointed shoes, which were clearly unsuitable for combat. However, since most Templars were actually employed in the more mundane administrative aspects of running a private army with a large banking and finance arm, the matter at hand was really that they expected all Templars to act like elite soldiers even if they were in fact bureaucrats or bankers.

spree in which they slaughtered Muslims and Christians alike. They must have felt rather foolish in the morning.

As the Crusades ended, the Templars fell out of favour. In the fourteenth century, King Philip IV of France got himself into rather a lot of debt to the Templars. Lending to kings was a tricky business. It was hard to refuse when they asked for a loan and hard to call in the debt if they did not pay it back. Philip's solution to his debt problem was simple: he abolished the institution to which he was indebted. He started by accusing the Templars of blasphemies and heresies, such as spitting on the cross and denying Christ. Then, one morning in 1307, he had hundreds of Templars arrested and tortured. When they duly confessed their crimes, he had them murdered.

The remaining Knights Templar in France went on the run. And they had a cunning plan to avoid detection. Philip had instructed his men to arrest anyone with a beard or a white tunic on suspicion of being a Templar. The Templars were one step ahead, however. They shaved, changed their clothes and ran for the border.

El Cid

Rodrigo Díaz was born near the city of Burgos in Northern Spain in 1043. He was a nobleman and a warrior. Southern Spain was occupied by the Moors – Muslims who had invaded from North Africa in the eighth century. In the years since his death, Díaz has become a popular folk hero in Spain. He was an accomplished military leader and the popular image today is of the ultimate chivalric knight. He is portrayed in epic poetry, drama and film as a Christian warrior who fought against the Muslim occupiers and inspired the re-Christianisation of Spain. He became known by the nickname given to him by the Moors – El Cid, The Lord.

Outside the Burgos Cathedral, where he is buried with his wife, is a statue of the legendary El Cid. The most notable feature of the statue is an absolutely enormous beard. The casual viewer might mistakenly believe that he is wearing a hairy blacksmith's apron that is tucked right up under his nose. It really is vast. His beard was something of a legend in itself.

The story went that, after his death, El Cid's corpse was able to perform miracles to help the Christian warriors. King Alfonso X used the legend of the Christian hero in the early thirteenth century. This time the target was not the Muslim occupiers, however, but the Jewish citizens of Spain.

Alfonso wrote *The First Chronicle of Spain* featuring the heroic El Cid. In this tale, El Cid's body was kept on display in the church of the San Pedro monastery after his death. It miraculously did not decay, and every year a feast was held on the anniversary of his death. One year, a Jewish visitor remembered that it had been said that nobody could pluck a hair from El Cid's beard and he wondered if he might take one. As he reached out to pick out a hair, El Cid's body leapt up and drew his sword. The Jewish man fainted then converted to Christianity in response. Chillingly, this was all part of Alfonso's anti-Semitic campaign, which would eventually lead to the expulsion of the Jews from Spain in 1492.

In reality, El Cid was not much of a hero. He was certainly a fine warrior, but he was more of a sword for hire than chivalric hero. He fought for Muslim rulers and then mixed Muslim and Christian alliances. He ultimately won a fiefdom for himself in Valencia. The legend of El Cid is almost entirely fictional. The only two real truths that have stood the test of time are a) that he was a fine military leader; and b) that he had a big beard.

It is likely that he picked up his beard from his Muslim friends, neighbours and enemies. While the Catholic Christians in Spain would more likely have been clean shaven, El Cid was happy to be a tough-looking warlord. Had El Cid really been a heroic Christian knight, he would most likely have been a lot more familiar with the razor than he actually was.

The beard of penitence

The sacking of Rome in 1527 was a largely domestic matter, with great importance in the issue of the destiny of facial hair. In the early 1500s, beards were making a bit of a comeback among the fashionable gentry of Europe. Slowly. It would be the sacking of Rome by Charles V's forces that would turn the tide in favour of the beard.

Charles V was Emperor of the Holy Roman Empire, constituting a slab of central and Eastern Europe. Charles saw himself as successor to the Roman emperors and wanted the Church to fall into line with his rule. Pope Clement was not so inclined, and a fight was sure to follow. Charles raised an army of twenty thousand Spaniards and Germans in 1527 and sent them to Rome to assert his authority. And by 'assert his authority', I of course mean to burn, torture, murder and rape the defenceless citizens of Rome, then steal whatever they could for themselves. It was devastating. Half the population of Rome was either killed or fled and never returned.

Pope Clement survived and concluded that God was punishing the people of Rome for their sins. He responded by growing a beard as a sign of his contrition and penance, following ancient Hebrew traditions. He encouraged others to follow his example, and by 1531 had removed the ban on clerical beards.

One of the priests in the papal court, Pierio Valeriano, embraced this and wrote the world's second book on the theology of beards, entitled *Pro Sacerdotum Barbis* (*In Support of Beards for the Clergy*).

Valeriano went further than Clement's act of penitence and went back to the arguments of the early church fathers on beards. He argued for a reinvigorated Church. It should be tough, macho and as hairy as God had made it. He also argued that beards had the medical benefits of expelling bad humours, preventing tooth decay and protecting the wearers from heat and cold. He (correctly) argued that the early church laws banning beards were fake news and priests should embrace the way of the Lord and go full beard.

Unfortunately for fans of the beard, Valeriano's book was not exactly a bestseller. Nevertheless, the increasing fashion for beards across Europe meant that some were willing to embrace his argument, even if the Church remained officially beardless. The timing was important in that it coincided not only with a fashion for beards, but also with a mood for reform in the Church. And the mood was gathering quite some pace.

Papal beards

One would imagine that, as the formal spiritual leader of the Western Church, the pope would have been the foremost observer of the principle of clerical shaving. You would think that the pope would have observed church law more strictly than any other believer. Well, actually, you would only think that if you knew very little about the history of the papacy. History records many popes whose standards fell a little below what would be expected. History also records popes whose behaviour was shockingly reprehensible by any civilised measure.

So after Clement grew his beard as an act of penitence, beards seemed to come and go from the faces of the popes who followed, depending on which way the wind was blowing. Most popes, whatever their moral fibre, were sticklers for their fashion sense. Occasionally a pope would appear determined to live within Catholic teaching and would shave, but just as commonly they did not. By the sixteenth century, when the Protestant Reformation exploded in Europe, there had been a run of twenty-five consecutive bearded popes.

Reformation beards

On 31 October 1517, it is said that Martin Luther famously nailed his *Ninety-five Theses on the Power and Efficacy of Indulgences* to the door of the church in Wittenberg, Germany, and started the Reformation in Europe.

It is widely accepted by historians, however, that this never happened. He certainly did send it to his local archbishop in Mainz, though, and this had pretty much the same effect. Luther did not stop with a letter to his local church authorities, however. With the help of the newly invented printing press, he began to issue pamphlets at a rate that had never before been imagined. The Protestant Reformation took hold most strongly in parts of Germany and Switzerland. Later, England joined in; after initially denouncing Luther's ideas, Henry VIII realised the advantages of breaking free from Rome, and England became the first country to be officially pope-free in Europe.

The Reformation had been building for some time. While it was Luther who lit the blue touchpaper and then kept pouring on petrol, the roots of the Reformation were broad and deep across European society. Life as a peasant in medieval Europe was unfathomably awful and the Church had become deeply corrupt, in league with the kings and nobles who used their power to keep the peasants in their place. Added to that, a rampant plague had been decimating the population of

Europe, and the impact of this had undermined the position of the official Church. Plague recurred regularly up until the mid-seventeenth century. So, by the 1500s, the peasants were revolting.[2]

The issue that got Luther's goat in those heady days of 1517 was the matter of indulgences. The common belief at the time was that, after death, believers would go to purgatory before they got into heaven. The length of time spent in purgatory would depend on how many sins they had committed. While you were in purgatory, these sins would be purged from you by the small matter of torture.

For this reason, the devout were keen to avoid as much time in purgatory as they possibly could. When the Church realised that it could provide the promise of time off purgatory in exchange for a fee, it discovered a revenue source that was too good to ignore.

The reason for Luther's concern was simple: this practice was unbiblical. He simply did not believe it to be part of the faith. He became increasingly strident in pursuing a version of Christianity based purely on what he read in the Bible and not on the traditions of the Church that could not be traced directly back to Scripture.

The obvious corruption involved in the sale of indulgences was too much for Luther, and he demanded that the church authorities take action – which, of course, they refused to do for financial reasons. And this set Luther and his followers on a course that would pit them against the Catholic Church and to the establishment of Protestantism.

---

[2] I can only apologise for including this hackneyed pun in this serious historical work. The important point to note is that the peasant classes were suffering hugely at this time and lost all respect for the obviously corrupt Church at a time of crisis. They were ready for a change.

The reformers of Europe had many issues with the Roman Church. And by 'many', I mean they had issues with almost everything.

After the attack on indulgences came Luther's trademark theological move: the doctrine of justification by faith. This is the argument that people can only be saved from their sins and accepted by God into heaven if they believe that Jesus died for them, since it is his death on the cross that puts us right with God. We cannot win God's favour by our good deeds.

Within Europe, the Reformation took hold in Germany and Switzerland most strongly, while France, Italy and Spain held to the Catholic faith. England waivered, until a young king found the need to consult the pope on religious matters all too inconvenient.

Just as with the schism between the Eastern and Western Churches in the eleventh century, the beard would play its role in the division of the Church in Europe in the sixteenth.

Henry VIII's beard

Henry VIII launched the Reformation in England, ostensibly in rejection of the corruption of the Catholic Church, but with the added benefit that, if he were to make himself Supreme Governor of the Church in England, he could grant himself an annulment of his marriage to Catherine of Aragon, for which he'd been pleading with the pope for years.

Earlier in his reign, Henry was seeking alliances in Europe. He had Spain in the bag after he married the Spanish king's sister, and now courted France. Europe was fractious and suspicious, but Francis I of France agreed to meet with Henry. There was a problem, though. A new Holy Roman Emperor was being elected, and Henry wanted to bide his time before meeting Francis. There was a major risk in postponing the visit if Francis should take offence. Henry needed to find a way of showing Francis that the delay was temporary and that he was fully committed to the visit at a later date. So he made a strange promise: he told Francis that he would not shave until he had visited the French king.

The logic is rather baffling, but seems to be that the inconvenience of a beard would be the motivation for Henry to re-arrange the visit as soon as possible. Henry's wife, Catherine, relentlessly lobbied her husband for its removal from the royal face. Her pleas were, of course, partly aesthetic and partly a result of her preference for alliances with Spain.

Henry relented and shaved, but a Venetian diplomat in his court let the cat out of the bag by sending word back to Francis. He was livid. Fortunately for Henry, his ambassador in France was legendary at sucking up to royals. Thomas Boleyn, who would later push his daughter into the king's path, smoothed things over by winning over Francis's mother, Louise. She commented, '[Love] is not in the beards, but in the hearts.'

The pressure was on for Henry, though. Among his least-bad qualities was his obsessive competitiveness. And he now knew that he would be meeting Francis in 1520, having promised to grow a beard, which he had not done, but which Francis very much had done. He could not bear the thought of turning up and having Francis rib him for having short and patchy fluff on his face.

So Henry grew back his beard. His portrait from his meeting with Francis, known as the Field of the Cloth of Gold, shows him with a respectably long beard. This he promptly shaved off when he got back, only to grow it again when he heard that the Venetian ambassador had described it as 'golden'.

Oh, Henry.

Henry's example led to others of the time following. Thomas More was Henry's closest associate, until Henry had him executed. More was resolutely Catholic and, after

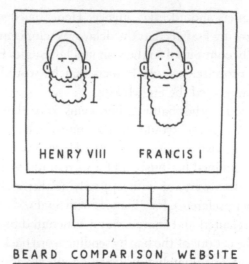

BEARD COMPARISON WEBSITE

burning a lot of Protestants, he was not prepared to go along with Henry's journey towards reform and the rejection of Rome. He could not sanction a divorce for Henry and so ended up where many of Henry's enemies did – facing an executioner. However, he was in many ways loyal to Henry, and when he walked to his execution he wore a long, grey beard. He was so proud of it, his final act was to save his beard from the executioner's axe, and his final words were a joke about it.

THOMAS MORE'S FINAL MOMENTS

About Nine he was brought out of the Tower; his Beard was long, his face pale and thin, and carrying a Red Cross in his Hand, he often lifted up his Eyes to Heaven; a Woman meeting him with a cup of Wine, he refused it saying, 'Christ at his Passion drank no wine, but Gall and Vinegar.' Another Woman came crying and demanded

some Papers she said she had left in his Hands, when he
was Lord Chancellor, to whom he said, 'Good woman,
have Patience but for an Hour and the King will rid me of
the Care I have for those Papers, and everything else.'
Another Woman followed him, crying, He had done her
much Wrong when he was Lord Chancellor, to whom he
said, 'I very well remember the Cause, and if I were to
decide it now, I should make the same Decree.'

When he came to the Scaffold, it seemed ready to fall,
whereupon he said merrily to the Lieutenant, 'Pray, Sir,
see me safe up; and as to my coming down, let me shift
for myself.' Being about to speak to the People, he was
interrupted by the Sheriff, and thereupon he only
desired the People to pray for him, and bear Witness he
died in the Faith of the Catholic Church, a faithful
Servant both to God and the King. Then kneeling, he
repeated the Miserere Psalm with much Devotion; and,
rising up the Executioner asked him Forgiveness. He
kissed him, and said, 'Pick up thy Spirits, Man, and be
not afraid to do thine Office; my Neck is very short,
take heed therefore thou strike not awry for having
thine Honesty.' Laying his Head upon the Block, he bid
the Executioner stay till he had put his Beard aside, for
that had committed no Treason. Thus he suffered with
much Cheerfulness; his Head was taken off at one
Blow, and was placed upon London-Bridge, where,
having continued for some Months, and being about to
be thrown into the Thames to make room for others,
his Daughter Margaret bought it, enclosed it in a
Leaden Box, and kept it for a Relique.

Hall's Chronicle. Vol. 2. S. 2.

It was a little surprising that Thomas More was so proud of his beard, in light of a fascinating dialogue he carried out over many years with William Tyndale.

Tyndale was something of a radical. He was at the cutting edge of the Reformation in England, introducing radical ideas like his translation of the Bible into English. More wrote a tract against Lutheran reformed Christianity, and Tyndale responded, while More was Henry VIII's chief minister. More could not resist rebutting the rebuttal, and the dialogue went on for years through the 1520s and 1530s.

Tyndale refuted many of the aspects of More's Catholic faith that he considered to be unbiblical, popish and unnecessary. One of these was shaving. In this passage, Tyndale becomes one of the first to argue for the role of women in public ministry within the Church – and also against beards:

We read that women have judged all Israel, and have been great prophetesses, and have done mighty deeds. Yea, and if stories be true, women have preached since the opening of the new testament. Do not our women now christen and minister the sacrament of baptism in time of need? Might they not, by as good reason, preach also, if necessity required? If a woman were driven into some island, where Christ was never preached, might she there not preach him, if she had the gift thereto? Might she not also baptize? And why might she not, by the same reason, minister the sacrament of the body and blood of Christ, and teach them how to choose officers and ministers? Poor women, how despise ye them! The viler the better welcome unto you. An whore had ye lever than an honest wife. If only shaven and anointed may do these things, then Christ did them not, nor any of his apostles, nor any man in long time after: for they used no such ceremonies.[3]

Elsewhere he criticised the practice of shaving that the Catholic clergy still obeyed as 'borrowed from heathen priests'. He was making the point that a priest is not a priest simply because he is shaved and anointed with oil. Truly radical stuff. The issue of priestly shaving would eventually be settled somewhat faster than the issue of admitting women to the priesthood.

Protestant reformed beards

Almost all of the reformers had beards. Shall we move on?

Well, that would not really be in the spirit of things, would it? Let us examine this partial truth a little more closely.

In England, Tyndale risked his life to publish a Bible in English before the Reformation had gathered enough momentum for it to be accepted. In 1528, he wrote that shaving 'is borrowed of the heathen' and that 'the shaven nation hath put Christ out of his room'.[4] He saw shaving as a Catholic invention.

Archbishop Cranmer steered Henry VIII along the path towards the English Reformation. He had built the case for the annulment of Henry's marriage to Catherine of Aragon and developed the concept of Royal Supremacy, placing the king at the head of the Church. In return, the family of Anne Boleyn convinced Henry to appoint Cranmer as Archbishop

---

[3] From Tyndale's snappily titled *An Answer to Sir Thomas More's Dialogue, The Supper of the Lord, After the True Meaning of John VI and 1 Corinthians XL*, 1528.

[4] William Tyndale, *An Answer to Sir Thomas More's Dialogue.*

of Canterbury. In portraits from the time of Henry's reign, Cranmer is shown clean shaven, as any pious priest of his time would have been. However, after Henry's death, his beard grew and acted as an indicator of the depth of reform he was able to introduce. Cranmer's most significant reforms came after Henry.

Cramner continued as Archbishop of Canterbury under Edward VI. Edward became king at just nine years old, having been raised a Protestant after the Reformation. Owing to his youth, the king's authority was exercised first through his uncle, who served as Lord Protector, and later through the Duke of Northumberland. Both were keen to push religious reforms on beyond Henry's ambition.

Among other things, Cranmer introduced the *Book of Common Prayer*, the doctrinal and liturgical basis of the Church of England. A portrait of Cranmer hangs at Lambeth Palace, the official residence of the Archbishop of Canterbury, to this day. The grey-haired Cranmer it depicts is near the end of his life and his beard is almost down to his waist. It remains a matter of contention whether Cranmer first grew his beard in mourning for Henry VIII. He was most certainly aware of the theological significance of the beard within the Catholic faith, however, its growth was undoubtedly a conscious sign of his rejection of Catholic tradition.

The approach of the reformers was to dispense with the unnecessary trappings of the Catholic faith, including the insistence on priests shaving, and to return to a faith based purely on the Bible. There was one striking exception, however.

As we noted earlier, the man who more than anyone can claim to have single-handedly started the Protestant Reformation is Martin Luther. Luther had no beard. He grew a beard briefly during a period when he was on the run from zealous Catholics attempting to arrest him (and burn him at the stake). But this merely indicates how surprised anyone would have been to see Luther with a beard. His portraits show him with a shadow of stubble, clearly demonstrating that he could have grown a beard if he had wanted to. But he did not. Like all complex characters from history, it is sometimes hard to get under Luther's skin. Or understand what was growing out of it.

As a young man, Luther had been an Augustinian monk. During this time, he had adopted the traditional tonsure. This involved shaving the top of the head and the beard. He would, of course, have been exposed to the traditional Catholic teaching on the beard. In his reforming days, Luther grew back the hair on the top of his head, married and fathered children. In doing so, he was casting aside much of the Catholic teaching he considered to be unbiblical. Yet he kept the habit of shaving all his life.

We have no writing from Luther on the subject of beards. This is extraordinary in itself, as he wrote prolifically on almost every theological topic you could imagine. So we can only speculate as to why he shaved.

One theory was simply that his generation shaved and that he grew accustomed to the habit. It is also possible that Luther's legendary arrogance played a part. The Catholic teaching from his days with the Augustinians included the view that priests would separate themselves from the sinful masses through their shaving. We heard earlier Abbot Burchard arguing that, while beards were symbols of manly virtues, the calling of the cleric was higher.

Luther did not believe that the clergy were a separate breed from the laity, however. He believed in the 'priesthood of all believers', so it is unlikely that he saw shaving as something that ought to be the exclusive preserve of priests. However, he certainly did see *himself* as uniquely placed in the world to interpret God's will. His attitude to anyone who disagreed with him was to slam them mercilessly, publicly and brutally.

Whenever Luther heard about something he disagreed with, whether by friends or enemies, he would rattle out a quick pamphlet to slam it and assert his authority. In his final work, entitled *Against the Roman Papacy, an Institution of the Devil*, Luther was in typical polemical form railing against Pope Paul III:

> Gently, dear Pauli, dear donkey, don't dance around! Oh dearest little ass pope, don't dance around dearest, dearest little donkey, don't do it. For the ice is very solidly frozen this year because there was no wind you might fall and break a leg. If a fart should escape you while you were falling, the whole world would laugh at you and say, 'Ugh, the devil! How the ass pope has befouled himself!' And that would be a great crime of lese majesty against the Holy See in Rome, which no letters of indulgence or 'plenitude of power' could forgive.

If you accept that Luther thought very little of anyone other than himself, it is possible that he had kept just a little of that Catholic teaching. Perhaps those with a higher calling were not all priests. But just a special one. Perhaps Luther did still see himself as a little separate.

Luther was a fascinating man. Some have questioned whether he had a personality disorder or suffered mental health issues. He was undoubtedly complex and contradictory. When it comes to his beard, we are left with a puzzle as to why he continued to shave after he had rejected so many other aspects of the Catholic faith. The most obvious reason was because he liked to be clean shaven. Perhaps there was a deeper reason, related to his self-perception and a desire to show his own unique position.

And with that exception noted, we can assert most assuredly that almost every other reformer had a beard. John Knox and John Calvin – or Jean Calvin as his mother knew him – were bearded. Huldrych Zwingli, who led the Reformation in Switzerland, was clean shaven, then grew a beard in later life. Heinrich Bullinger, close ally of Zwingli and chief minister in Zurich after Zwingli's death, had an absolutely majestic flowing beard. It was shaped like an equilateral triangle, originating from his nose.

From a theological perspective, the reformers had a point. They were discarding the theological baggage the Catholic Church had acquired for which they could not mount a defence from the Bible. However, for the populace, this newfound freedom meant more than just a theological shift. It meant that the solid foundation they had of the teaching of the Church was now a theological free-for-all. The reformers agreed that everyone should read the Bible for themselves in their own language. They all agreed on personal salvation through faith. So the effect was to make religion much more of a personal belief system than a corporate and collective one. It meant that people began to freestyle. They could read the Bible, understand it and challenge the views they heard from the pulpits. From here, Protestantism would split, split again, then keep on splitting, as ever-smaller groups argued that their leaders had fallen into theological error.

The same was true of their facial hair. Without the authority of the Catholic Church telling them how to style their beards, the new beard styles were about to take off, and fashions would soon come and go like the breeze.

In his epic book, *A History of Christianity*, Diarmaid MacCulloch argues that the reformers had another reason for growing their beards. One of the key reforms introduced was the abolition of the requirement for priestly celibacy. Protestant priests got married. This coincided with a renewed interest in a matter that has continued to obsess the Church right up to today: sex.

Traditional Catholic teaching argued that all sex was essentially sinful and that abstinence was superior; Erasmus taught that the ideal marriage involved no sex. The reformers argued that this does not come from the Bible. For them, marriage was a healthy and holy estate, and theologies around sex developed in ever more elaborate ways. Part of this came with an emphasis on the distinct roles of men and women in the Church, society and the family. And what better way to show the distinct masculine nature of the male of the species than for him to grow a beard.

During the period leading up to the Reformation, the Catholic Church found itself in a strange position. It had managed to get its hands on a huge amount of temporal power and was able to control the lives of many ordinary people through its requirement for pilgrimage, tithes and the purchase of indulgences. Yet, in many ways, its moral authority was lower than it had ever been. The self-evident corruption of the Church dramatically undermined the extent to which its social teaching was accepted.

On the issue of beards, we see periodic rulings against beards from popes, archbishops and priests, yet they came and went in the papal court along with the fashion.

The Van Dyke

As we explore the story of how beards became the preserve once again of the religiously devout of Europe, we must make a special place for a style that is perhaps the most dashing of all: the Van Dyke. This is the style of a goatee and moustache combination, but with the cheeks shaved. It was creatively named at the time after the Flemish painter Van Dyck, who wore such a thing and painted a number of Europe's nobility in the same style. It became the absolute height of fashion for a short period.

In England, the Van Dyke was the style of Charles I. As a result, it went slightly out of fashion when Charles's beard became detached from his body, along with the rest of his head, at the hands of Oliver Cromwell. Cromwell himself is shown in portraits wearing the Van Dyke, although in other portraits he adopted the more puritanical, full-face, close shave.

The association with Charles was not strong enough to kill the Van Dyke in itself, however. Other notable patrons of the style include the Holy Roman Emperor Ferdinand II, and Cardinal Richelieu. The important Reformation theologian Arminius was also a fan.

The style came and went fairly quickly. With the Restoration in England in 1660, French styles came into fashion, and the royalty and nobility of Europe dropped the Van Dyke.

The pattern was now set. Clerics and noblemen no longer had to worry about the religious significance of their beards. They were free to follow the fashions of the day. In a sense, this marked one of the first defeats for religion in its war with culture in Europe. Even the Catholic Church gave in. Eight popes in a row adopted the Van Dyke, from Urban VIII in 1623 to Innocent XII in around 1700, abandoning the tradition of shaving and going along with the more fashionable style of the day.

PART V

BEARD SCIENCE

9

Beard Sexism, Racism and Semen on the Brain

By this point in our story, we have surveyed the religious history of beards from the dawn of time to somewhere in the middle of the seventeenth century. We have seen times when beards were compulsory. Times when they were banned. Times when shaving was seen as essential to approach the gods. And times when shaving was seen as a terrible offence against God. We have also seen how the beard has been an important part in the identity politics that has included division along religious lines. We have seen how the Eastern and Western Churches divided and used the issue of the beard as one to pick a fight over. We have seen how key figures in the Protestant Reformation signalled their split from Rome by growing beards.

And now we shall see how succeeding generations continued to use the issue of facial hair as a way to signal a departure from whatever came before them.

Beliefs and opinions about the science of beards are far from a historical curiosity. These beliefs originated before the birth of Christianity in a society that thought that those with beards were a superior species to those without. That does not mean all men, however. It specifically draws the boundary at

European men as the superior species. This is ironic, since
they also believed that the relative hairlessness of humans was
one of the things that distinguished them from animals. What
it reveals is that those who wrote the science in days gone by
often tended to conclude things that they wanted to conclude.
The beard would therefore become an instrument of sexism
and racism.

It is worth noting that this is the context within which the
Church was doing its theology around the role of women.
No wonder they struggled their way so slowly towards
equality.

The evolution of the beard

A simple biological question: why do those with a Y chromosome sprout hair from the lower half of their faces once they
have gone through puberty? The mechanics of this process
can be described, but the heart of the question remains elusive.

A number of theories have been put forward by evolutionary biologists to try to explain why men should have evolved
with this trait. Darwin was the first to theorise about the
evolutionary purpose of the beard in *The Descent of Man*.[1]
His theory was that the beard acted akin to a peacock's
feathers. By demonstrating that he could grow a long, full and
lustrous beard, a man would attract a mate who was impressed
by this display of follicle virility. Others have suggested that
the beard was not there to attract mates so much as to scare

---

[1] We must note that Darwin himself wore an enormous beard, so
perhaps his thinking on this was influenced just a tiny bit by the
predominant social expectation of his time that a beard was a
sign of masculinity and virility.

off other males by making the dominant male appear bigger, tougher and more aggressive.

In order to test these theories, scientists with nothing better to do have examined whether there appears to be any emotional response to beards from either men or women. The theory was that an evolutionary benefit of beards in attracting mates should result in a residual effect today in that males with beards should be more attractive to females. Similarly, if the reason was to appear more aggressive and frightening to other males, a residual effect should be traceable today in men's responses to others with beards.

Tests were devised to show women a range of male faces, some with beards digitally added and some with them removed. First, women were asked to rate the attractiveness of each face to see whether the beard did indeed make the male face more irresistible.

Similarly, men were shown a range of faces and asked to indicate whether they thought the men were strong, aggressive, weak or something else.

Sadly for these scientists, the results showed that there appeared to be no relationship whatsoever between beardedness and attractiveness, scariness or any other personality traits that would result in an evolutionary advantage. Some studies appeared to show a link, but these were quickly contradicted by other studies with the opposite results.

The plain fact appears to be that reactions to beards are almost entirely dictated by personal preference and influenced by the fashions and cultural associations of the day. There simply is no single universal response that could explain an evolutionary basis for beard growth.

We can be sure that beard scientists will continue the quest, but it does leave us with the possibility that there is no evolutionary advantage to having a beard, and that it is more evolutionary hangover than asset: our more-primitive ancestors were hairy and this hair was lost, with the exception of certain areas, including the beard. The problem with this theory is that where hair did remain in other areas – and we will not dwell on these bodily regions here – this does appear to result in an evolutionary advantage. Furthermore, virtually none of our surviving evolutionary cousins have hair around their mouths. Chimpanzees, for example, have hair covering their entire bodies *except* around their mouths, and on the palms of their hands and on their feet.

Unless some radical new thinking emerges, there appears to be no reason for the existence of beards. Like nipples on men, or whatever it is that makes people ticklish, beards appear to serve no purpose, but have survived because they do not cost men anything either.

It is just possible that, at the deepest biological level, beards are totally and utterly pointless. If this is the case, it is astonishing the extent to which beards have influenced human culture and history. From the earliest recorded history of humankind, we seem to have believed that the state of our facial hair was of primary significance to our gods and acted as a symbol of our character. This continues in various forms today.

FAKE NEWS ALERT : FAKE NEWS ALERT : FAKE NEWS

A surprising amount of junk science has been written on the origin of beards. It is hard to sift through the chaff to find the wheat of genuine scientific investigation, but your humble author has done this for you to save you the effort.

If you see any of the following theories advanced in the name of science, you are perfectly entitled to turn your nose up and declare it fake news:

1. 'Beards offered warmth to early humans.' The heat retention of a beard that hangs down from the face is minimal. Thick, all-over body hair would have been a more obvious response to the need for warmth.

2. 'Beards offered protection to males who got into fights.' To test the level of protection offered by a beard, anyone proposing this theory should attach a fake beard then ask a friend to punch them in the face. They will soon find that it offers no protection whatsoever. Worse than that, they may find it is actually a liability in hand-to-hand combat, as it is easily grabbed.

3. 'Beards provided protection from harmful ultraviolet light in a natural form of sunblock.' There is some evidence that facial hair blocks some UV rays, but there is no evolutionary reason why this benefit would be given exclusively to men, and the effect is so small as to be negligible.

4. 'Men dribble and scoff their food like pigs, so beards help to hide this.' Okay, there is some truth to this one.

FAKE NEWS ALERT : FAKE NEWS ALERT : FAKE NEWS

Beard science

Scientific beliefs[2] around beards began, alongside most systematic beliefs, among the ancient Greeks. Hippocrates,

---

[2] The term 'belief' is the correct term to use when examining science for most of its lifetime. Observation and scientific method was mixed with philosophy and religion to produce scientific opinions for most of the history of science.

who lived in the fifth and fourth centuries BC, is often called the father of medicine and was the first to compile a broad 'scientific' approach to the body and illness. He considered many topics, including hair, baldness and beards. It took some time before his writing was considered authoritative, but from around the second century AD his views held sway among consensus opinion in the ancient world. They came back into fashion in Europe with the Enlightenment and fascination with all things classical and were taught in European universities until the middle of the seventeenth century.

For Hippocrates and those who followed, the body was believed to be constituted of four 'humours' which dictated the behaviour and wellness of the individual. The humours were blood, yellow bile, black bile and phlegm. Each produced characteristic effects, and illness was the result of an imbalance in these humours.

Everyone had all four humours, but the balance between them was the key. Where one was elevated, it would result in various illnesses and physical characteristics. Blood was considered hot and wet and would result in thick, luxuriant, abundant, often wavy hair. Yellow bile, however, was believed to be hot and dry and would result in curly, thin or fine hair. Balding was common in men with an excess of yellow bile, and they would have blond or reddish hair. For those who had heightened black bile, they would have thick, straight, dark or dark brown hair. The beard would be sparse, though. The more phlegmy man could enjoy blond or light brown hair and light facial hair.

These humours were mixed with 'vital heat', which gave the body life. It was heat that caused food to be digested, and it produced a kind of life force that was pumped around the body by the heart. Heat became concentrated as semen, which was so potent it could produce new life when in the woman's womb. The theory came from the simple observation that living things are warm, then they go cold when they die.

Hippocrates wrote a classic case study of Phaethousa of Abdera, the wife of Pytheas. Pytheas went away and Phaethousa promptly stopped menstruating, grew a beard, then died. The conclusion seemed obvious: without the husband having sex with her, her menstrual blood was not being moved around the body, since it was having sex with a man that kept her highly fertile body open. With the build-up of menstrual blood that resulted, a build-up of heat began. This caused the beard to grow, but then it all became too much for the fragile female body, and she died. An excess of heat in a woman's body made it more like a man's body. Because of this theory, some believed that a spontaneous sex change could occur if sufficient heat were to build up. Others disagreed and believed that death would result before the sex change fully took place.

Because it was thought that beards were caused by heightened heat in certain parts of the body, it was argued that men are hairier than women owing to their having more heat. Their larger frames and bigger heads also explained why they were cleverer – more heat, of course. Those big, strong guys generated more heat in general, but also around the mouth specifically. And this is where the theory gets really strange.

The ancients believed that semen was stored in the head. It explained why the head was so hairy – the hair acted as a kind of release valve for the heat that came from this vital substance housed within. During sex, the semen then travelled down through the body, but would get a little stuck around the chin, as this is a particularly tricky area for semen to navigate. This is why the male chin would become hairy too.

Using this robust scientific basis, it was argued that hair was a sign of virility. It also explained why men started to go bald at the same time they started having sex. Having sex effectively transferred the hair from the head to the chin. This is why, even until recently, bald men were considered to be particularly virile and masculine.

Your esteemed author will only remind you that these are not his theories, but those of some profoundly ill-informed scientists of the ancient world. One reason we took this day trip from reality is because this argument was used by none other than Pierio Valeriano, whom you will remember we met in the papal court of St Clement, back in the sixteenth century. In his version of natural law theology, he argued that this was all as God intended and clerics should embrace it. Beard theology, based on ancient Greek pseudo-science.

Some have also argued that this theory of semen in the head lies behind one of St Paul's most enigmatic writings. In 1 Corinthians, Paul is writing to one of the churches he founded and says at length that men should not cover their heads when they speak in church, but women should. He concludes:

> *Judge for yourselves: Is it proper for a woman to pray to God with her head uncovered? Does not the very nature of things teach you that if a man has long hair, it is a disgrace to him, but that if a woman has long hair, it is her glory? For long hair is given to her as a covering. If anyone wants to be contentious about this, we have no other practice – nor do the churches of God.*
> (1 Corinthians 11:13–16)

This has been the subject of debate for centuries. Since male hair is just as long as female hair when left to its own devices, in what way does 'the very nature of things' teach us that men should have short hair? One argument is simply that Paul is referring to cultural norms in his society. Some take it further to suggest that women with short hair would be mistaken for prostitutes, who would have their heads shaved, and men with long hair would be considered effeminate. This does not quite ring true, as a number of cultures in Paul's day considered men with long hair to be the tough warriors.

When we look back at the theory of semen in the head, we can see that Paul may be considering the widespread view in the Greek-influenced world, namely that nature teaches us that if men have long hair it will drain their semen from their head too much and they will become impotent, while women with short hair will be unable to draw the sperm towards the womb and they will become barren.

The argument also goes that long hair on a woman is effectively part of her reproductive equipment. This would explain why Paul requires women to keep their hair covered during worship: it is effectively a form of testicle. Long hair is given to women as a fertility aid to draw up semen.

Well, it's a theory.

Beard racism

Racism as a scientific endeavour began in earnest in the seventeenth century. At this point, 'scientists' began to argue for the biological differences between people on which they could base their racism. Historically speaking, humankind appears to have had few qualms about enslaving, murdering and seriously mistreating people it sees as different. However, the seventeenth century saw the age of global travel combining with an Enlightenment desire for rationalistic explanations for the natural world, which moved racism into another gear.

In 1684, François Bernier, a French doctor, traveller and personal physician to an Indian prince, described four species of man. Among the key characteristics that distinguished these species was, of course, the beard. Europeans and North Africans were one species and had lush, flowing beards. Black

Africans were another, who had scant beards of 'three or four hairs'. The people of East Asia he considered to be white people but with 'flat faces, small flat noses, little pig's eyes' and, again, distinguished from Europeans by their scant beards. His final species were the Lapps, or Laplanders, whom he described as 'animal-like' in appearance.[3]

As late as 1852 we see Charles Hamilton Smith writing about human differences based on beard type in *The Natural History of the Human Species*, distinguishing the 'Caucasian or Bearded Type' from the 'Mongolic or Beardless Type'.

By the mid-eighteenth century, the same logic was applied to the indigenous people of North America, noting that they belonged to a lower class of human, with some arguing that the lack of beard growth showed that they were, in fact, a separate species altogether.

In 1786, Richard McCausland, an army surgeon, wrote in the *Philosophical Transactions of the Royal Society of London* that 'it has been advanced by several travellers and historians that the Indians of America differed from other males of the human species in the want of one very character-istic mark of the sex . . . that of a beard'.

Now, such physical descriptions could be considered a harmless historical curiosity, had it not been part of a much wider, more pernicious and evil attitude. The desire to create classes of people and rank them allowed not just racism, but also the justification for slavery, colonialism and the subjuga-tion of peoples.

Not everyone accepted beard-based racism. Naturalist Richard Bradley identified five 'sorts of men' in 1721, with Europeans and Americans distinguished solely by their beards and two 'sorts' of black races distinguished purely by the texture of their hair. However, Bradley explicitly argued that

---

[3] 'A New Division of the Earth', *Journal des Sçavans*, 1684.

there was no moral or social distinction between any people. He concluded, 'I suppose there would not be any great difference [between different races]; if it was possible they could be all born of the same parents, and have the same education, they would vary no more in understanding than children of the same house.'[4]

Nevertheless, the attitudes that developed through the Enlightenment and after were deeply racist. They 'justified' Western colonialism and slavery on the basis of more-advanced and civilised peoples subjugating lesser people and bringing a civilising effect – and beards were part of that story.

When it came to the Church, these attitudes were central to the evangelical drive through the colonies. It was the moral responsibility of all good Christian people to bring the civilising influence of Western Christianity to the heathen nations. It was an attitude that lasted a surprisingly long time. In 1930, the Lambeth Conference brought together all Anglican bishops in the worldwide Anglican Church, and they resolved at the end of the meeting that . . .

> . . . partnership [between countries] must eventually follow as soon as two races can show an equal standard of civilisation. Accordingly, the Conference affirms that the ruling of one race by another can only be justified from the Christian standpoint when the highest welfare of the subject race is the constant aim of government, and when admission to an increasing share in the government of the country is an objective steadfastly pursued.

In other words, British colonialism could be a good thing if done correctly.

---

[4] Richard Bradley, *Philosophical Account of the Works of Nature*, 1721.

Beard sexism

Immanuel Kant is one of the central figures in modern philosophy, writing in the late eighteenth century. His writing was hugely important in the fields of ethics, religion, law, aesthetics, astronomy and history. He argued that perpetual peace on earth could be achieved through universal democracy and international cooperation, and that this is the ultimate trajectory of history. By the standards of his day, he would have been considered enlightened in his attitude to women: he believed them to be virtuous and beautiful. But he did not believe they were equal to men in other ways; for Kant, men were intellectually and morally superior. So when female writers, such as the classicist Madame Dacier or the physicist Émelie du Châtelet, began to publish papers and promote their ideas, he responded that scientific learning by women ran counter to the laws of nature. A woman 'might just as well have a beard, for that expresses in a more recognisable form the profundity for which she strives'.[5] Kant believed that the beard showed man's superior intellectual ability.

During the nineteenth century, the thinking that led to beard racism and beard sexism was based on the science of physiognomy: the idea that the study of the physical form could reveal truth about the moral and intellectual character. Physiognomy was accepted wisdom since it had been established by the ancient Greek philosophers. Pythagoras went as far as to use it to vet students before accepting them to study with him. Physiognomy went briefly out of fashion from the mid-sixteenth century when it had become associated with fraudsters – just imagine. However, it came back, and in the eighteenth century, Enlightenment thinkers were reviving all

---

[5] Immanuel Kant, *Observations on the Feeling of the Beautiful and Sublime*, 1764.

things ancient and looking for new sources of wisdom from natural sciences.[6] This included the growth in phrenology – the idea that the bumps on the head could show the behavioural characteristics of the person. Based on physiognomy, it was evident that more-masculine faces, the hairiest ones, revealed the underlying character traits that they believed distinguished the genders.

As the nineteenth century wore on, the cause of gender equality gathered momentum, and some men responded to this by seeking to reinforce the differences between the genders. This is one reason why beards made such a comeback in the 1800s.

When women began to demand the right to vote, the beard once again became a symbol of male superiority. A wealth of literature was produced by the anti-suffrage movement, including cartoons designed to mock and denigrate the suffragettes. One such card shows an ugly suffragette with an absurdly long nose talking to a bearded lady at a circus. The suffragette is shown saying, 'How do you do it?' The implication is that suffragettes really just want to be men, and the bearded lady is their hero.

Even today, it is argued that there is a link between beards and sexism. One recent study, entitled 'The Association

---

[6] Physiognomy is the fake science that just will not die. Despite being debunked repeatedly over the centuries, it persists even today. It persists in the digital era in attempts to use artificial intelligence (AI) to examine faces and derive character traits. A 2009 study claimed to have detected a link between the width of ice hockey players' faces with the number of fouls committed, and therefore was associated with aggression levels. Another 2017 study claimed that AI could detect sexual orientation using facial recognition. Neither result has been proven. Physiognomy also persists in our language – when we refer to 'highbrow' or 'lowbrow' topics, we are using the language of physiognomy.

Between Men's Sexist Attitudes and Facial Hair', examined the attitudes of 500 men and ranked them for sexism.[7] They hypothesised that 'men with relatively sexist attitudes would be more likely to allow their facial hair to grow than men with less sexist attitudes'. They thought that, since beards carry connotations of masculinity, those who choose to grow beards might be attempting to consciously enhance their own perceived masculinity, and that this desire for perceived masculinity may be associated with views of traditional gender roles and sexist attitudes. The study rated participants by facial hair status and attitudes to women. Sadly, the bearded men scored markedly worse than the non-bearded participants. The authors concluded that bearded men are indeed more likely to have hostile attitudes to women, with just one-third of bearded men who participated being considered 'non-sexist'.

Bearded ladies

This seems an opportune moment to briefly segue into a discussion of women with beards.

We have seen that most men throughout history have considered their facial hair to be a mark of masculinity and male superiority. The beard has often symbolised virility and strength. Jews and early Christians considered the beard an important symbol of their faith. So you might assume that women with the ability to grow beards would be considered specially blessed, would you not? They would surely be considered selected by God for a special status, to be elevated above less-hairy women and men alike.

---

[7] Julian Oldmeadow and Barnaby Dixon, 'The Association Between Men's Sexist Attitudes and Facial Hair', Archives of Sexual Behaviour, May 2016.

Of course not, you silly billy. This is a man's world, and while the men have been in charge, women certainly would not have been elevated to special positions. Women with beards have consistently been considered 'freaks' and treated appallingly.

We have come across history's most famous fake-bearded lady in the Pharaoh Hatshepsut already, and discussed the fake beards of the women of Argos. However, since modern humans have evolved, some women have also had the ability to grow beards, and this has been a source of fascination and curiosity. While this ability is rare, various studies have estimated that between 5 and 15 per cent of women have what is considered to be 'excessive' hair in 'male patterns', known as the condition hirsutism. It was back in 1961 that Ferriman and Gallwey published their landmark study on the subject, which gave birth to the Ferriman–Gallwey scale for rating the thickness and pattern of female hair. Today an increasing movement is attempting to remove the taboo from this perfectly natural and common condition.

In the fifth century BC, Herodotus recoded in *Histories* that the people of Halicarnassus lived in fear of the priestesses at the temple of Athena growing beards, as this was considered a disastrous omen of terrible things to come. We can only speculate as to why they were so worried about this.

Several bearded ladies have left their mark on history, and we will celebrate them now in the hope that the taboo around female hair will go away, along with the foolish assumptions that men are inherently better than women.

The *Topographia Hibernica*: history's first-recorded bearded lady

The *Topographia Hibernica* was a record of the people and landscape of Ireland, written shortly after the Norman Conquest. It was written by the appropriately named Gerald of Wales. Gerald had a pretty low opinion of Ireland. To be fair, it was a land that had not developed its culture and civilisation in the same way that Anglo-Saxon England had during the period before the Norman Conquest. The document reads like an exploration of a remote and exotic land. He includes an account of a bearded lady, the first recorded in history:

> Duvenald, King of Limerick, had a woman with a beard down to her navel, and also, a crest like a colt of a year old, which reached from the top of her neck down her backbone, and was covered with hair. The woman, thus remarkable for two monstrous deformities, was, however, not an hermaphrodite, but in other respects had the parts of a woman; and she constantly attended the court, an object of ridicule as well as of wonder. The fact of her spine being covered with hair, neither determined her gender to be male or female; and in wearing a long beard she followed the customs of her country, though it was unnatural in her. Also, within our time, a woman was seen attending the court in Connaught, who partook of the nature of both sexes, and was an hermaphrodite. On the right side of her face she had a long and thick beard, which covered both sides of her lips to the middle of her chin, like a man; on the left, her lips and chin were smooth and hairless, like a woman.

Saint Wilgefortis: the bearded lady saint

The legend of Wilgefortis arose in the fourteenth century. She is considered the patron saint of women seeking liberation from abusive husbands.

The story of Wilgefortis goes that she was a teenager of noble birth when pledged by her father in marriage to a pagan king. Since Wilgefortis was deeply committed to her faith, and had taken a vow of chastity, she prayed earnestly to God to be delivered from the marriage. The Lord duly answered her prayers by the miraculous gift of a lustrous beard that sprouted overnight. This made her repulsive to her betrothed, who duly called off the wedding. Sadly, it wasn't all good news for Wilgefortis, as her pagan father had her crucified in his anger at the whole affair.

We can be pretty confident that this biography is a work of fiction, as there are many variations of the story, sometimes with Wilgefortis given a different name. Her feast day was removed from official calendars on the grounds that she is a fictional character, but she is still listed in some reference works on the saints.

Ânna Macallane: bearded lady to the king

The portrait of Ânna Macallane adorns the collection of the National Portrait Gallery. We know little about her, but the description tells us that she was born in the Orkney Islands of Scotland in 1615 and was presented to King Charles II in 1662. Under her portrait is the following rhyme:

> Though my Portraiture seems to bee
> A Man; my sex denys me so;
> Nature hath still variety;
> To make the world her wisdom known.

Well said, madam.

Annie Jones: Barnum's bearded lady

Annie was the world's most famous circus bearded lady. She was born in 1865 and started her career touring with P. T. Barnum's circus, having had hirsutism from childhood. She was enlisted in the circus by her parents when she was just nine months old and was billed as the 'infant Esau' after the famously hairy biblical character. By the age of five she had a moustache and sideburns and went on to have a full, long beard. Annie was frequently photographed, and her portrait was widely circulated. She became a national figure. Annie married twice, but ended her life as a widow. During her life, she tried to stop the word 'freak' being used to refer to circus attractions like her.

Good on you, Annie.

Conchita Wurst: not a bearded lady

In 2014, Conchita won the Eurovision Song Contest for Austria with her song 'Rise Like a Phoenix'. This text will make no judgement on the musical quality of the entry. Conchita's appearance is striking as a typically female character in every way, besides a full dark beard.

Conchita is actually the stage persona of Thomas Neuwirth, who identifies as a man and uses masculine pronouns when referring to Thomas. However, he also performs under the persona Conchita Wurst and uses feminine pronouns when referring to Conchita. Although Thomas considers himself a drag artist rather than a transsexual woman, Conchita's victory, including high scores from a number of former Soviet states, was considered an important milestone in the acceptance of transgender and transsexual people, and she has been an inspiration to women with hirsutism. There are now a number of prominent women who are refusing to cut, shave, wax or bleach their facial hair and seeking to end the taboo that exists around it.

Beard psychology

One question that we have not yet considered is why men grow beards. We have looked at those with religious motivations, but even the most generous reading shows that this has only ever been part of the motivation. In practice, the desire of a man to wear a beard has always been a mixture of identity politics and the desire to be part of a 'tribe', the assertion of masculinity, fashion and the following of social norms.

When we fast-forward to our current time, many of these factors have fallen away. It is no longer the case for many people that they come from a group or nation which is predominantly either bearded or clean shaven. In most of the world today, men are free to choose. Neither is the assertion of traditional masculinity such an appealing trait in the current climate.

Psychologists have tried to look at the phenomenon of why men freely choose beards. To start with, the obvious reason to grow a beard is a desire to become more attractive. A number of studies have been conducted to see whether this strategy may work. In 1973, undergraduates' faces were rated, and bearded men were seen as better-looking, more masculine, mature, dominant, self-confident, courageous, liberal, nonconforming, industrious and older. Result for the beards.

Another very similar study in 1991, however, rated clean-shaven men as younger, more attractive and more sociable. Two more studies in 2017 resulted in a victory for the bearded in one but no difference between beards and non-beards in another. A number of studies have shown that the most attractive look for men tends to be a heavy stubble, so somewhere between beard and non-beard.

When you add it all up, there is no consistent result.

What psychologists *have* concluded is that opinion about beards depends on the culture. Where beards are common, growing one no longer marks a man out as distinctive and interesting. This was tested recently by scientists who showed participants in a study a series of pictures of men with beards, then asked them to rate the attractiveness of a clean-shaven man. Then they repeated the exercise the other way around. The result was that the one who bucked the trend got better results.[8]

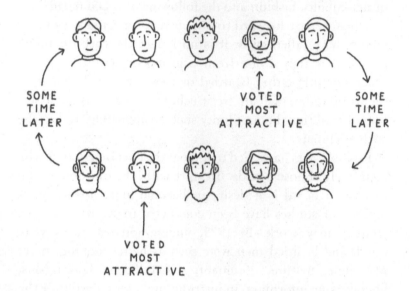

SOME
TIME
LATER

VOTED
MOST
ATTRACTIVE

SOME
TIME
LATER

VOTED
MOST
ATTRACTIVE

So perhaps the swing in fashion for and against beards is a pull between two forces. One force drives men to become distinctive, but they then become trendsetters and a crowd mentality pushes others to copy them. When critical mass is achieved, the pendulum swings with a desire for distinctiveness by reversing the trend.

When the Church looks at the fashionable trends of the day, there may be an inbuilt tendency to resist new and distinctive thinking, so it has tended to oppose the facial hair innovators. When beards have been dominant within the culture, they

---

[8] Zinnia J. Janif, Robert C. Brooks and Barnaby J. Dixson, 'Negative frequency-dependent preferences and variation in male facial hair', *Biology Letters* Volume 10 Issue 4 (Royal Society Publishing).

have been seen as normal, natural, God-given and holy. Where shaving has been the norm – such as in the early Roman Church – that is the state that has been seen as natural, respectable and respectful to the Lord. What is fascinating is the lengths Christians have gone to in making this case. They have invented histories, including stories about St Peter, and created whole theologies to explain what they think God thinks about how hairy a man's face should be.

PART VI

BEARDS ARE BACK

10

Shaving Revival

The beard is very much back. But how did we get here? From almost total extinction, beards have become the mark of a young and culturally connected Christianity. A form of Christianity that is at the cutting edge of contemporary culture has not only revived the beard, but also made it a central mark of this new kind of hipster Christianity. The revival of beards has been a roller coaster ride of fashion, war and the invention of the safety razor.

During this period, old theological ideas have come back into fashion, and shifts in society have taken the Church along with them to lead us to where we are today – a facial-hair free-for-all. The traditional theological foundations of the past have been thrown away and we are left searching for meaning in our facial hair. Beards in the Church today are more likely to signal a cultural meaning than a theological one, and the old questions about whether God favours a hairy face or not have been consigned to the past.

Evangelical beards

The Protestant reformers established firmly that beards were no longer anathema. The Catholic Church could no longer demand shaving, and beards came back. In fact, many popes and senior clerics in Rome were already bearded while the Reformation was kicking back against their anti-beard theology.

Like all revolutions, the Reformation eventually ate itself, however. The newly reformed Church itself became corrupted. As reformed churches became the established churches in a number of European countries, the compromises needed to combine temporal and spiritual power took their toll.

By the beginning of the 1700s, the Church in England was at a desperately low ebb. The morals of the nation had hit new low after new low, and drunkenness and gambling were common pastimes. The ruling classes were getting rich by trading slaves and opium. In the nation's parishes, Christianity was barely visible. Sir William Blackstone, a politician and judge, toured London's churches and observed that he 'did not hear a single discourse which had more Christianity in it than the writings of Cicero'.[1]

At this point, facial hair was taking new and innovative forms. British traders and soldiers who made their fortunes in the Indian subcontinent with the East India Company found themselves alongside bearded and moustachioed locals. When they returned home to England, it was the height of fashion to demonstrate your worldliness with an exotic facial styling. By 1800 we see the emergence of whiskers (expansive hair just on the sides of the face), pork chops (long sideburns cultivated into the shape of a pork chop) and all manner of new creative styles.

And in this heady mix of heathen England and creative facial hair, a Christian revival broke out. It started with the preacher George Whitefield, who roused large groups with his fiery preaching. John and Charles Wesley followed, speaking directly to the working man and woman. They were initially ridiculed as 'enthusiasts' and later became known as evangelicals. The Wesleys founded the Methodist movement.

---

[1] Charles J. Abbey, John Henry Overton and John Roland Abbey, *The English Church in the Eighteenth Century*, 1896.

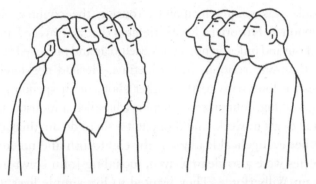

THE AWKWARD MOMENT THE LEADERS
OF THE PROTESTANT REFORMATION MEET THE
LEADERS OF THE EVANGELICAL REVIVAL

Methodism was a straight-talking, no-nonsense kind of Christianity. The Wesleys told people that they needed to be saved from their sins, to work hard, to study the Bible and generally to take life much more seriously than they were. George Whitefield and the Wesleys had faces as smooth as a newborn baby's bottom. They despised the vanity that went into the excessive beard styling of the day. For them, a well-nurtured beard showed that the man concerned had succumbed to the sin of vanity.

According to a contemporary account, Wesley's lack of beard caused an incident at one of his meetings. A heavily bearded man approached Wesley and told him, 'Sir, you can have no place in heaven without a beard! Therefore, I entreat you, let yours grow immediately!' He went on to argue that this would save him vital time in the morning which could be put to better use in doing God's good work. Wesley responded that shaving daily gave him time for reflection before starting the working day.

In contrast to his bearded assailant, Wesley saw the beards of his day as a sinful extravagance: spending time and money on one's appearance when one should have been working towards the building of God's kingdom on earth as it is in heaven. And Wesley was a tireless worker after this cause. His preaching schedule was simply incredible, touring the country almost continuously. Historians have estimated that he travelled around four thousand miles on horseback each year and preached around forty thousand sermons in his lifetime. He had absolutely no interest in long trips to the barber shop, or in spending time oiling, waxing, combing and shaping a handlebar moustache. He wanted to get to work, and thought it a sin to do anything else.

Other evangelical leaders of the eighteenth and nineteenth centuries were also clean shaven, including John Newton and William Wilberforce. They wanted to live simple lives, dedicated to the Lord's work.

PERSECUTED FOR WEARING A BEARD

A story from the Boston Daily Globe *in 1884 shows just how far beards had fallen out of fashion in parts of America.*

Joseph Palmer was a bearded US army veteran who served in the War of 1812 and retired to the life of a farmer. He grew up in the village of Notown, Massachusetts. He was described as a kindly man.

Religious but tolerant. He was always rather eccentric. At the age of forty he decided to emulate Jesus and Moses by growing a beard. At this time in America only Jewish Americans wore beards.

In 1830, he moved his farm to the small town of Fitchburg, Massachusetts. When he arrived, he found that he was the only bearded man in Fitchburg and was considered an eccentric on account of his strange looks.

The extent of the persecution he faced was extraordinary. The children of the town threw stones at him and called him 'Old Jew Palmer'. He found himself thoroughly harassed, being shouted at in the streets by children and adults alike. The minister of the church in Fitchburg refused him Communion, so Palmer grabbed the chalice and shouted, 'I love my Jesus as well, and better than any of you!'

The minister told him he looked like the devil, and he replied, 'Mr Trask, are you not mistaken in your comparison of personages? I have never seen a picture of the ruler of the sulfurous regions with much of a beard, but if I remember correctly, Jesus wore a beard not unlike mine.'

One day he was seized in the street by a group of men who attempted a forced public shaving. In the struggle that followed, Palmer cut his assailants' legs and was arrested. Judge David Brigham ordered him to pay a $10 fine, $40 in court fees and a $700 bond. Palmer chose prison instead and was jailed for more than a year.

Even in prison he did not escape persecution. The prison guards beat him and starved him. He became sick. His fellow captives tried to cut off his beard. As a result, he began to write letters of complaint about his treatment in jail. When he was eventually released from prison, he became a campaigner for prison reform and against slavery. He founded the Fruitlands Commune with Louisa May Alcott, then farmed the land and opened it up to the homeless, radicals and writers.

He eventually died in 1875, by which time beards were very much back in fashion. His tombstone read, 'Persecuted for wearing the beard'.[2]

---

[2] 'Persecuted Joseph Palmer', *Boston Daily Globe*, 14 December 1884.

Just as almost all the leaders of the Protestant reformation were bearded, so all the leaders of the evangelical revival were clean shaven. Both had their reasons, but in truth they were simply reacting to what had come before. The reformers wanted to show a visible change from the beardless clerics of the Roman Church, while the evangelicals wanted to show their difference from the creatively bearded clergy of the Church of England. The one exception was Luther, who wanted to show he was different from everyone.

By the start of the nineteenth century, once again the fashion had swung in the other direction and beards were very much out. In some places, beards were almost entirely absent.

Beards of war

Just as beards came to the brink of extinction, however, their comeback was triggered by a war. And a religious war at that. One of the bloodiest wars of the nineteenth century, it began with an argument over a key.

Christians in the Holy Land had long been in the minority and had established an uneasy agreement regarding access to the holiest sites in Christendom. The central argument was between the Roman Catholics in Palestine and the Eastern Orthodox Christians. They argued over who was in charge of the sacred places. The trouble was not just that they argued, but also that they had some rather irresponsible backers.

In the Catholic corner was Napoleon III, eager to restore prestige and glory to France. In the Orthodox corner was Tsar Nicholas I, keen to expand Russian territory and influence as the Ottoman Empire declined and receded. The British and the Ottomans sided with the French in an effort to keep Russia in check.

The churches had actually come to an agreement, but Napoleon and Nicholas were not going to back down. Each appointed someone as 'protector' of the Christians in Palestine, in possibly the most ironic use of the word 'protector' in history. Both tried to back up their argument with a show of force.

Napoleon deployed the eighty-gun warship *Charlemagne* to the Black Sea, while Tsar Nicholas deployed his fourth and fifth army corps along the River Danube in Wallachia.

The Crimean War was the result, from 1853 to 1856. Around one million souls would perish before it ended. The vast majority of the deaths came from disease. And this was the reason why the beard made a dramatic comeback.

Crimea was the war of Mary Seacole and Florence Nightingale. It was when medical practitioners first began to understand basic hygiene methods. Disease was rampant and soldiers and nurses alike sought reasons why disease and infections were spreading. While beards had been banned in the army before the war, at that time the only method of shaving was to spread shaving soap over the beard area and shave with a cut-throat razor.

One of the inevitable results of this method of shaving is the occasional nick. This mattered little back home, but in a war zone with rampant infection and disease, soldiers found that their shaving cuts were either slow to heal or commonly became infected. On top of that, supplies of razors and shaving soap became impossible to get hold of, so shaving became an even more hazardous activity when they were forced to improvise. Similar conditions were experienced during the American Civil War in 1861–1865, which led to a reintroduction of facial hair almost simultaneously on both sides of the Atlantic.

By the time Charles Dickens visited America in 1867, as possibly the most famous man on the earth, he was sporting a 'doorknocker beard' (a moustache joined with a long, goatee beard). His image was in every newspaper in the country and the fashion for creative facial hair was at its height. Fashions come and go, however, and by the 1880s in the US and in England beards were only worn by the older generation.

The beard that launched a career

One of the most influential preachers of the second half of the 1800s was Charles Spurgeon. He was converted into an evangelical faith in a Wesleyan chapel in 1850 at the age of just fifteen. He was an inspired preacher from a very young age. He became a Baptist and founded the Metropolitan Tabernacle, which became one of the largest churches in London.

While still a teenager, Spurgeon was speaking alongside two other ministers in his home town of Colchester. After he spoke, the other two turned to attack Spurgeon. He wrote about the event in his autobiography:

> One of them, in particular, was very personal and also most insulting in his observations, specially referring to my youth, and then, in what he seemed to regard as a climax, saying that it was a pity that boys did not adopt the scriptural practice of tarrying at Jericho [a reference to a Bible story from 2 Samuel 10] till their beards were grown before they tried to instruct their seniors.[3]

Spurgeon asked the moderator for an opportunity to respond, in order to correct their interpretation of the biblical text:

> I reminded the audience that those who were bidden to tarry at Jericho were not boys, but full-grown men, whose beards had been shaved off by their enemies as the

---

[3] Charles Haddon Spurgeon's Autobiography (originally published by Fleming H Revell Company, 1898) Vol I, p. 298.

greatest indignity they could be made to suffer, and who were, therefore, ashamed to return home until their beards had grown again.

Luckily for Spurgeon, one of the audience members was a deacon at New Park Street Chapel in London. He was so impressed that he invited Spurgeon to London to preach. Spurgeon would later write how that event 'became, in the hand of God, the means of my transference from Cambridgeshire to the metropolis'.

Spurgeon was a product of the evangelical revival, but in just fifty years the beard fashions had changed yet again. By 1850, almost every respectable gentleman in England had a beard. It was no longer considered an act of vanity, but one of basic respectability. Spurgeon commented that wearing a beard was 'a habit most natural, scriptural, manly and beneficial'.[4] And he lived the words he preached: with a fine, short, cropped beard.

Beard theology had come full circle. Spurgeon had finally reached the same point as Augustine had almost two thousand years earlier: he saw beards as natural and a sign of a healthy manliness, while following in Christ's footsteps.

The Great War

While it was war that reintroduced beards to a generation, the First World War played a significant part in killing off beards for another generation.

During the early twentieth century, coinciding with the patent granted to King Camp Gillette[5] for the disposable

----

[4] Charles Spurgeon, *Lectures to My Students*, 1875, 1:134.

[5] Yes, that was his real name.

razor in 1904, scientists began to understand the existence of bacteria. Beards became a target of suspicion regarding their hygiene status and began to be banned in places of work that relied on rigorous hygiene standards.

As the fashion for beards began to wane, now backed up by the new science of bacteria, a generation of men was called up to fight in a truly dreadful war. Between 1914 and 1918, around six million British men fought in the Great War. This was around 15 per cent of the entire population of Britain.

One aspect of the Great War that made it so terrible was the invention of a new form of weapon that was both deadly and terrifying: mustard gas. The first chemical weapons were crude and simply involved releasing deadly gas canisters when the wind was blowing towards the enemy. The results were awful.

Soldiers were trained to put on gas masks at a moment's notice when the gas alarm was raised. And one thing that could risk the seal around the mask was a bushy beard. So being clean shaved could literally be a matter of life and death. War taught a generation to shun the beard.

When we reflect on the impact of war on beard history, we should also remember that the Church was in the midst of these conflicts. The famous nurses of the Crimean war, led by Mary Seacole and Florence Nightingale, were supported by large numbers of religious nurses – nuns who answered the call to care for injured soldiers.

On the front lines, army chaplains were an essential part of any military operation, providing support and comfort to troops in extreme conditions. In Crimea, chaplains and religious nurses spent the majority of their time in the hospitals, caring for those who were injured and sick. In the First World War, chaplains would be with the men on the front line, as well as in support, and they would witness the horror of mustard gas attacks first hand.

11

Modern Beard Rebels and Pioneers

At this point in the story, it would be a temptation to believe that controversy over whether or not beards are God's cup of tea are a thing of the past. The foolish Christians of centuries past wasted their time on all that theological nonsense over facial hair. Nobody would do that today. Would they?

One of the most influential pastors in the United States is unquestionably Rick Warren. He is pastor of Saddleback Church, a vast 'mega-church' with an average weekly attendance of around twenty-two thousand in 2017. His programme for personal growth and church growth has been followed by millions across the world.[1]

As well as being a natural leader, Warren is a bit of a rebel. While at high school, Warren started a Christian club, indicating the kind of leader he would become. But if you had passed him in the street, you would have thought he was a follower of John Lennon rather than Jesus. He styled himself on the trendy 'Jesus Movement' which came out of California in the 1970s and blended traditional Christianity with quasi-hippy youth culture.

He grew up in the Southern Baptist Church. This is the largest denomination in America and is traditionalist and

---

[1] Rick Warren, *The Purpose Driven Life: What on Earth Am I Here For?* (Zondervan, 2002).

conservative. One of the rites of passage for young Southern Baptists was to obtain a lay preaching licence. Warren was up before the committee in his church who would decide whether he was ready to preach to them. They tested him on his knowledge of Scripture and his theology, which he passed with ease. However, the committee was concerned that he looked rather like a hippy. The hippy movement was a challenge to the Church, with its advocacy of free love and a culture of drug taking. Warren managed to defend himself with the argument that his fashion sense would help him connect with young people.

Warren founded Saddleback in California with his wife Kay in 1980. He pioneered a church growth strategy based around being 'seeker sensitive'. To a wardrobe full of Hawaiian shirts, Warren added a goatee and moustache. In 2013 he hosted a beard competition at his church. The taboo around facial hair had truly been eliminated.

Another important figure in twentieth-century Christianity was Eugene Peterson. Peterson is best known for creating *The Message*, a paraphrase of the Bible. He wrote many influential books and was a major figure in the global Church until his death in 2018.

Peterson also had a beard. His look towards the end of his life was that of a friendly grandfather: white-haired and wrinkled, with prominent white teeth when he smiled – which he did a lot. In a television documentary about his life he told a story about wanting to become a monk when he was young. He had been a bit of a loner as a child and felt he did not fit in with other children. He was committed to his faith, so becoming a monk seemed a good option. One issue did not quite work for him, though: he wanted to grow a beard. Like Warren a few years later, this was deeply frowned upon, and so Peterson waited until it was a little more socially acceptable.

The antipathy to beards in 1960s and 1970s Christianity was so deep that some seminaries went so far as to ban them. As with previous beard persecutions, the issue was only partly to do with the existence of facial hair. It was more to do with the idea that wearing a beard was a symbol of membership of a cultural group of which the Church did not approve: hedonistic hippies.

Hipster Christianity

The latest phenomenon in the sphere of ecclesiastical facial hair has come with the emergence of hipster Christianity. This was memorably explored in Brett McCracken's book of the same name.

A hipster church usually looks nothing like a church from the outside. Young, trendy people bounce inside and are greeted by a mixture of exposed brick interior, atmospheric mood lighting and a band on stage with as much equipment as the average U2 concert. There are plenty of tattoos on display. After singing songs in a time of worship, the pastor emerges – if you have not been there before you would not pick them out of the crowd as the pastor, most likely young and trendy again – to lead a sermon full of modern cultural references.

Naturally, in such a group of people, the beard-to-man ratio will be high. These beards will probably have recently been trimmed by a professional barber and carefully oiled each day.

In his book, McCracken not only identifies this phenomenon but also poses a much more profound question about it: is Christianity meant to be cool? Are Christians meant to take the central message of the gospel and update its packaging to make it more appealing to those who are young and otherwise disengaged? Or are they meant to teach them the traditions of the Church?

This author will not attempt to navigate these particular choppy waters but will merely observe that the logic behind this largely bearded hipster movement appears to be similar to that behind the Protestant reformers, Rick Warren and Eugene Peterson. As we heard earlier, the apostle Paul said:

> *To the Jews I became like a Jew, to win the Jews. To those under the law I became like one under the law (though I myself am not under the law), so as to win those under the law. To those not having the law I became like one not having the law (though I am not free from God's law but am under Christ's law), so as to win those not having the law. To the weak I became weak, to win the weak. I have become all things to all people so that by all possible means I might save some.* (1 Corinthians 9:20–2)

Perhaps, if Paul were here today, he would say that to the hipsters he became like a hipster so as to win those in skinny jeans eating avocado on toast for Christ.

Of course, it is not only hipsters and rebels who wear beards in the Church today. Special mention must be made of one particular bearded archbishop. Rowan Williams was awarded the prestigious title of 'Beard of the Year' by the Beard Liberation Front in 2008.[2] Some have argued that his beard is inspired by his respect for Orthodox Christianity, although it is equally possible that he just does not like shaving.

---

[2] Let's just say that prestige is in the eye of the beholder.

A PREACHER CONNECTING WITH HIS FLOCK

The former Bishop of London, Richard Chartres, grew his beard in the 1970s ahead of a retreat to the Coptic monastery of St Bishoi, in the Wadi el-Natrun in Egypt. He wrote later that he felt so at home there that he kept the beard as a constant reminder. In 2016, while still Bishop of London, he spoke out in praise of East End hipster priests, saying that their beards were 'to be applauded' and that those of many other faiths would respect the bearded man as a holy man. He argued that the beard could be a tool for evangelism.

We now see priests and bishops wearing beards for a variety of reasons, but rarely are these reasons theological.

CONCLUSION

The Final Word

If you have made it to this point in our story, my dear reader, then I salute you. If you have skipped to the end to see how the story finishes, then I am afraid I am not terribly impressed with you. Nevertheless, it seems that, after having looked through the entire recorded history of humankind to pull out the story of beards and religion, we should attempt to draw some conclusions from what we have learned.

The first is that we have seen how beard theology has been important as part and parcel of the context in which it was written. Factors like the scientific theories of the day, which believed that semen stored in the head was the reason for hair growth, or the basic assumption that men were a superior form of creation to women, were important. These factors led male theologians through church history to debate the role of beards, starting from a place we would not recognise. As these preconceptions have changed, the theological debate around beards has all but disappeared, and we have almost forgotten that it ever took place.

Meanwhile, other theological debates rage. Clerical celibacy was a later invention than beard theology, and remains in place within the Roman Catholic Church today, still a matter of debate. It is difficult not to wonder how the basic assumptions of the theologians of the past have influenced their conclusions on issues we regard as contemporary controversies, such as the debates over the role of women in Church leadership or around issues of sexuality. Perhaps future generations will look back at the disputes of today and treat them with the same curious bemusement with which we have surveyed the beard theologies of the past.

But this work is not about those issues. The final word, therefore, must be to consider the ultimate question of beard theology: should good Christians shave or not?

On the one hand, we can see that to imitate Jesus we should embrace the bushy beard. On the other, Paul's instruction to be 'all things to all people' would lead those of us in predominantly shaved societies to take up our razors.

Another answer presents itself: God really does not mind. In the Bible we find the prophet Isaiah speaking to the Israelites, who were wondering why God did not seem impressed by their religious observance and fasting. He told them that you should not act all religiously one day, then oppress your neighbour the next. The same logic applies to any attempt to impress God with our beards. So our final word will be from Isaiah, probably the most bearded man of all. Instead of worrying about fasting (or facial hair), he tells us what God really cares about:

> Is not this the kind of fasting I have chosen:
> to loose the chains of injustice
> and untie the cords of the yoke,
> to set the oppressed free
> and break every yoke?
> Is it not to share your food with the hungry
> and to provide the poor wanderer with shelter —
> when you see the naked, to clothe them,
> and not to turn away from your own flesh and blood?
> Then your light will break forth like the dawn,
> and your healing will quickly appear;

then your righteousness will go before you,
and the glory of the Lord will be your rear guard.
Then you will call, and the Lord will answer;
you will cry for help, and he will say: here am I.
If you do away with the yoke of oppression,
with the pointing finger and malicious talk,
and if you spend yourselves on behalf of the hungry
and satisfy the needs of the oppressed,
then your light will rise in the darkness,
and your night will become like the noonday.
The Lord will guide you always;
he will satisfy your needs in a sun-scorched land
and will strengthen your frame.
You will be like a well-watered garden,
like a spring whose waters never fail.

(Isaiah 58:6–11)

HODDER &
STOUGHTON

Hodder & Stoughton is the UK's
leading Christian publisher,
with a wide range of books from
the bestselling authors in the UK
and around the world ranging from
Christian lifestyle and theology to
apologetics, testimony and fiction.
We also publish the world's
most popular Bible translation
in modern English, the New
International Version, renowned
for its accuracy and readability.